Communications
in Computer and Information Science   1553

More information about this series at https://link.springer.com/bookseries/7899

Bing Qin · Haofen Wang · Ming Liu ·
Jiangtao Zhang (Eds.)

CCKS 2021 - Evaluation Track

6th China Conference
on Knowledge Graph and Semantic Computing, CCKS 2021
Guangzhou, China, December 25–26, 2021
Revised Selected Papers

Springer

Editors
Bing Qin
Harbin Institute of Technology
Harbin, China

Ming Liu
Harbin Institute of Technology
Harbin, China

Haofen Wang
Tongji University
Shanghai, China

Jiangtao Zhang
Tsinghua University
Beijing, China

ISSN 1865-0929   ISSN 1865-0937 (electronic)
Communications in Computer and Information Science
ISBN 978-981-19-0712-8   ISBN 978-981-19-0713-5 (eBook)
https://doi.org/10.1007/978-981-19-0713-5

This Springer imprint is published by the registered company Springer Nature Singapore Pte Ltd.
The registered company address is: 152 Beach Road, #21-01/04 Gateway East, Singapore 189721, Singapore

Preface

This volume contains the papers presented at the evaluation track of CCKS 2021: the China Conference on Knowledge Graph and Semantic Computing, held during December 25–26, 2021, in Guangzhou, China.

CCKS is organized by the Technical Committee on Language and Knowledge Computing of the Chinese Information Processing Society. CCKS was formed by the merger of two previously held relevant forums, i.e., the Chinese Knowledge Graph Symposium (CKGS) and the Chinese Semantic Web and Web Science Conference (CSWS). CKGS was previously held in Beijing (2013), Nanjing (2014), and Yichang (2015). CSWS was first held in Beijing in 2006 and was the main forum for research on Semantic Web technologies in China for a decade. Since 2016, CCKS has brought together researchers from both forums and covered a wider range of fields, including knowledge graphs, the Semantic Web, linked data, natural language processing, knowledge representation, graph databases, information retrieval, and knowledge aware machine learning. It aims to become the top forum on knowledge graphs and semantic technologies for Chinese researchers and practitioners from academia, industry, and government.

The CCKS technology evaluation track aims to provide researchers with platforms and resources for testing knowledge and semantic computing technologies, algorithms, and systems, to promote technical development in the field of domestic knowledge, and to foster the integration of academic achievements and industrial needs. The CCKS 2020 technology evaluation track attracted 4056 teams to participate, forming a highly influential competition. This year, following discussion and selection by the General Chairs, Program Committee Chairs, and Evaluation Track Chairs, CCKS 2021 set up five evaluation topics and 14 evaluation tasks:

Topic 1: Domain information extraction
Task 1: Address text analysis
Task 2: Knowledge extraction for process information in communication domain
Task 3: Portrait of scholars in web documents
Task 4: Medical named entity and event extraction for Chinese EMR

Topic 2: Passage-level information extraction
Task 5: General fine-grained event detection
Task 6: Passage-level event extraction and event causality extraction in the financial domain

Topic 3: Link prediction
Task 7: Link prediction over phenotype-drug-molecule multilayer knowledge graph

Topic 4: Knowledge graph construction and KBQA
Task 8: Information extraction in insurance domain and reasoning Q&A for operator knowledge graph

Task 9: Inference of entity type for general encyclopedia knowledge graph
Task 10: Construction of knowledge graph in military vertical domain for military UAV system
Task 11: Generation of Chinese medical dialogue containing entities
Task 12: Content understanding of Chinese medical popular science knowledge
Task 13: Q&A on knowledge graph in life service domain

Topic 5: Multimodal Q&A
Task 14: Knowledge enhanced video semantic understanding

We also set up bonuses and issued certificates for the top three teams of each task. At the same time, we selected the "innovative technology award" for different tasks, which encourages and rewards the use of innovative technologies.

We attracted over ten thousand teams for the competition. We encouraged the teams to submit evaluation papers. Finally, 17 teams submitted their evaluation papers in English. All the papers came from teams ranking in the top three in their competition tasks. After a rigorous peer review by experienced researchers, all 17 papers were accepted after revision for this volume of proceedings.

December 2021

Bing Qin
Haofen Wang
Ming Liu
Jiangtao Zhang

Organization

CCKS 2021 was organized by the Technical Committee on Language and Knowledge Computing of the Chinese Information Processing Society.

General Chairs

Bing Qin   Harbin Institute of Technology, China
Zhi Jin   Peking University, China

Program Committee Chairs

Haofen Wang   Tongji University, China
Jeff Pan   University of Edinburgh, UK

Evaluation Track Chairs

Ming Liu   Harbin Institute of Technology, China
Jiangtao Zhang   PLA 305 Hospital, China

Evaluation Track Program Committee

Bing Qin   Harbin Institute of Technology, China
Haofen Wang   Tongji University, China
Ming Liu   Harbin Institute of Technology, China
Jiangtao Zhang   Tsinghua University, China
Haichao Zhu   Harbin Institute of Technology, China
Tao He   Harbin Institute of Technology, China
Zihao Zheng   Harbin Institute of Technology, China

Contents

A Biaffine Attention-Based Approach for Event Factor Extraction

Jiangzhou Ji[✉], Yaohan He, and Jinlong Li

China Merchants Bank Artificial Intelligence Laboratory, Shenzhen 518000, China
{jesse,heyh18,lucida}@cmbchina.com

Abstract. Event extraction is an important task under certain profession domains. CCKS 2021 holds a communication domain event extraction benchmark and we purposed an approach with the biaffine attention mechanism to finish the task. The solution combines the state-of-the-art BERT-like base models and the biaffine attention mechanism to build a two-stage model, one stage for event trigger extraction and another for event role extraction. Besides, we apply several strategies, ensemble multi models to retrieve the final predictions. Eventually our approach performs on the competition data set well with an F1-score of 0.8033 and takes the first place on the leaderboard.

Keywords: Event extraction · NER · Biaffine attention

1 Introduction

There are many kinds of processing knowledge in the communication field, such as hardware installation (installation and operation steps of base station equipments), parameter configuration (configuring parameters related to the network element opening and docking), integrated commissioning (network element opening, debugging and function verification), fault handling (repairing faults during network element opening or normal operation), etc. Among them, fault handling process knowledge is particularly important.

In the communication operation and maintenance process, the fault process knowledge is sorted through "events" to present the logic of the fault occurrence to the user, providing fault troubleshootings and recovery solutions, and guiding the front line to deal with existing network faults. In the process of collating fault knowledge, "event extraction" is an important way to sort out the fault context, troubleshoot and recover the system.

The challenge of "event extraction" in the communication domain lies in the complexity of the communication service, which contains the domain long words, ambiguous events, element sharing, etc. To address this challenge, CCKS 2021 organized the benchmark task of process knowledge extraction competition for communication field.

The CCKS 2021 communication domain process knowledge extraction task aims at extracting event trigger words and event arguments from free text, that

© Springer Nature Singapore Pte Ltd. 2022
B. Qin et al. (Eds.): CCKS 2021, CCIS 1553, pp. 1–10, 2022.
https://doi.org/10.1007/978-981-19-0713-5_1

is, given text T, extract all event sets $\mathbf{E}$ in text T, and for each event e in $\mathbf{E}$, extract trigger words (including words, positions and classifications) and roles (including words, positions and classifications) of $\mathbf{E}$ from text T. Figure 1 gives an example of event extraction for this task.

Sample1

Input： 将直放站小区半径参数由2000m改为10000m

Output： {"trigger": ["SetMachine", 14, "改为"], "argument": [["Object", 1, "直放站小区半径"], ["InitialState", 9, "2000m"], ["FinalState", 16, "10000m"]]}

Sample2

Input： XX小区晚上8点之后苹果终端接入5G网络失败

Output： {"trigger": ["SoftHardwareFault", 14, "接入"], "argument": [["Subject", 10, "苹果终端"], ["Object", 16, "5G网络"], ["State", 20, "失败"]]}

Fig. 1. Example of communication domain process knowledge extraction

In this task, precision (P), recall (R) and F1 measure (F1-score) are used to evaluate the recognition effect of event elements. The micro average is used to calculate the F score, that is, the elements (trigger words and roles) of all samples are used to calculate P and R together. The trigger word of the event and each role are statistical items.

Compared with the traditional event extraction task, the hardest technical challenge of this task lies in the overlap of elements, which means the same trigger or argument may belong to different events. To address these challenges, we proposed a joint learning method based on the biaffine attention mechanism model.

The rest of the paper is organized as follows: Sect. 2 reviews some related works; Sect. 3 discusses our approach; Sect. 4 presents the experiment implementations and results; Sect. 5 concludes the paper and sketches directions for future work.

2   Related Works

Event extraction is to predict the event category, event trigger word, element corresponding to the trigger word, and the arguments of the corresponding element for a given document. Correspondingly, schema-based event extraction mainly includes four tasks: event classification, trigger identification, argument identification and argument role classification [1]. In fact, event extraction tasks can be transformed into classification tasks, sequence annotation tasks or machine reading tasks [2]. In this task, since we need to identify the event elements corresponding to the event type based on the word level, we turn it into a NER (Named Entity Recognition) problem.

According to different technical implementation methods, event extraction method can be divided into the following two groups:

Pattern Matching Methods. Event extraction based on pattern matching is mainly divided into supervised pattern matching methods and weakly supervised pattern matching methods [3]. The pattern matching event extraction method has excellent performance in the domain event extraction task, but the production of the template requires a lot of manpower and time, and the template is limited to the domain background, which is difficult to apply in the general domain event extraction task.

Kim et al. introduced the WordNet semantic dictionary [4], using semantic framework and phrase structure for event extraction. Ellen et al. developed the AutoSlog-ST system based on AutoSlog [5], which does not need to label all event elements in the corpus, just label the event type, and then use the pre-classified corpus to automatically learn the event mode. Jifa proposed a domain general event pattern matching method IEPAM [6], which divides event extraction patterns into semantic patterns, trigger patterns and extraction patterns, and achieved excellent results in flight accident event extraction in MUC-7 corpus.

Machine Learning Methods. Especially deep learning and neural networks, have become the mainstream technology for event extraction [7–11]. Because the machine learning method does not require expert knowledge, it is easier to implement than the pattern-based method, and it has strong scalability and can be transplanted to multiple fields [12]. Traditional machine learning methods extract the semantic features of the text, and then build a model for event ex-traction. Limited by the ability of feature representation, the effect is often uneven.

The neural network method models the event extraction as an end-to-end system, using word vectors containing rich language features as input to automatically extract features, without requiring or minimal reliance on external NLP tools, avoiding the tedious work of manually designing features.

Nguyen and others used two-way LSTM to extract semantic features in sentences, and then combined sentence structure features to extract event trigger words and event elements at the same time [13]. Wang et al. proposed an event extraction model based on a generative confrontation network, called the confrontation-neural event model (AEM) [14]. Zhang et al. proposed a new neural network-based transformation model for joint prediction of nested entities, event triggers and their semantic roles in event extraction [15].

In recent years attention mechanism has become a key technique to improve performance of NLP models, and the pointer network structure has become the mainstream method in NER problem especially in the nested situation. However the general pointer networks encode start and end pointer together, in [16] the authors propose an attention mechanism considering start and end pointer simultaneously using a biaffine operation which achieve a better result in NER task.

3   Approach

In this section, we'll describe the overview, the design of each stage and the strategies we applied for improvements.

3.1   Overview

We regard this communication domain knowledge extraction task from text as a NER task overall like [17]. That means NER models extract the text spans and classify them with defined event trigger and argument labels.

According to the CCKS 2021 Dataset, we choose a biaffine attention based pointer network connected to the BERT-based model, since biaffine pointer networks could handle with nested spans while BERT-based model outperforms in semantic comprehension [16,18].

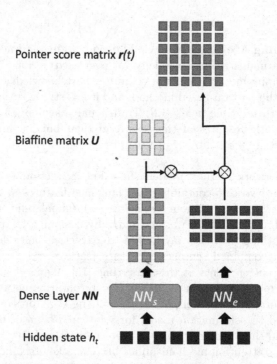

Fig. 2. The flow of biaffine attention mechanism

In detail, the BERT-based model receives input text T and we retrieve its output embedding h_t of each token t. Using h_t to connect to two pointer networks, noted as NN_s and NN_e, is for predicting the head and tail of the spans separately, computed as:

$$h_s(t) = \text{NN}_s(h_t) \tag{1}$$
$$h_e(t) = \text{NN}_e(h_t) \tag{2}$$

Finally the score matrix of span, with number of categories C is computed as:

$$r(t) = h_s(t)^\top \mathbf{U} h_e(t) + b \tag{3}$$

where $\mathbf{U}$ is a $d \times (C+1) \times d$ tensor (1 for non-entity category; d is the hidden size of h) as the transformer matrix, and b is the bias item. And applying the position constrain of the head and tail, we could rank the predicted spans, as:

$$y'(t) = \arg\max r(t) \tag{4}$$

After ranking of the predicted spans, the model will output the final predictions. And the flow of the biaffine attention is illustrated in Fig. 2.

Since this knowledge extraction task defines as: given the input communication domain text T, the model should output the event triggers and corresponding event arguments, we split this task into two stages: Stage-1 and Stage-2. Stage-1 defines as: given the input text T, model outputs triggers t_i and their categories c_i. Stage-2 defines as: given the input text T, the trigger t_i and corresponding category c_i, model outputs the argument spans a_i and their label regarding to t_i. And the overview structure of our approach is shown in Fig. 3.

Apparently, each stage could be regarded as multi-class classification problem for tokens. Hence we apply the uniform softmax cross-entropy shows below proposed in [19] as the loss function to optimize our models.

$$L = \log\left(1 + \sum_{(i,j)\in P_\alpha} e^{-r_\alpha(i,j)}\right) + \log\left(1 + \sum_{(i,j)\in Q_\alpha} e^{r_\alpha(i,j)}\right) \tag{5}$$

$r_\alpha(i,j)$ is the biaffined score of span from i to j. P_α is the set of heads and tails of category α, and Q_α is the set of heads and tails of category non-α or non-entity. Note that only $i \le j$ should be considered. This loss function has no category imbalance, because it does not turn multi-label classification into multiple binary classification problems, but a pairwise comparison between the target category score and the non-target category score. With the help of the good nature of logsumexp operator, it automatically balances the weight of each equation item. Moreover, it proves improvements in several NLP tasks.

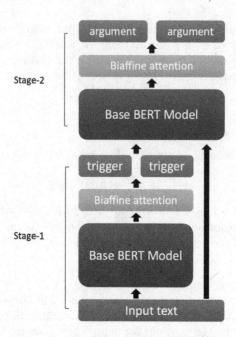

Fig. 3. The overview of our approach

3.2 Design of Stages

Each stages share the BERT-like model part, and the BERT-like model is pretrained on a large scale Chinese corpus. We'll describe the detailed design and hyper-parameters of each stage above.

Stage-1. This stage model is like a classical BERT NER model. Tokenized raw input text feeds into the BERT-like part. Two full-connected layers are connected to the last hidden embedding states of BERT-like model, and followed by a biaffine layer, which outputs the classification logits for each token t_i.

Since the Stage-1 model plays the role of event trigger extractor, the objective NER categories are defines as: **IndexFault, SoftHardwareFault, CollectData, Check, SettingFault, ExternalFault, SetMachine, Operate** and **non-entity**.

Stage-2. The global structure of Stage-2 is like Stage-1, the differences are the input and output categories. Since the Stage-1 predicts the event trigger, the Stage-2 takes the raw input text, predicted trigger category, predicted trigger span and predicted trigger start position as the input, while they are joined by the [**SEP**] token. As for the output, the objective NER categories are all possible event argument keywords: **Data, FinalState, Index, InitialState, Network, Object, Owner, Reference, Setting, Source, State, Subject** and **non-entity**.

3.3   Our Strategies

To outperform in this CCKS 2021 benchmark, we apply some strategies to the model implementation, the training process and the output predictions.

Multi Base Model Choice. We replace the semantic extractor part with several pretrained BERT-like models including *ELECTRA-large*, *MacBERT* and *RoBERTa-large*, which are pre-trained on a large scale mixed Chinese corpus.

Apply Adversarial Learning. During the training phase, we apply adversarial learning to improve the robustness of model to the adversarial samples. We choose projected gradient descent method to implement adversarial learning. The PGD attack is a variant of BIM (Basic Iterative Method) with uniform random noise as initialization, which is recognized to be one of the most powerful first-order attacks.

Model Ensemble. We ensemble the predictions of Stage-1 from several base models by voting strategy to get the best event trigger predictions. And as same, we ensemble the predictions of Stage-2 to get the final predictions.

Output Postprocessing. Since the classification of Stage-2 has no restrictions on event argument categories, we remove the predictions whose argument category doesn't pair the trigger category. Furthermore, we remove the predictions whose trigger-argument span has a long distance, since the position of the trigger and its argument is usually near.

4   Experiments

In this section, we'll describe the data set in the CCKS 2021 task and experiment results of our approach.

4.1   Data Set

The data set provided in the competition mainly comes from the fault handling cases disclosed by Huawei, including about 15k pieces of training text and 2k pieces of verification text. The event type to be extracted contain a total of 8 categories, the statistics of each type and its role is shown in Table 1.

We calculated the text length of the data set, and found that over 99.6% text are shorter than 160 characters meanwhile the average length is 26.87. Therefore, we choose 160 as our max length of input token and truncate the rest characters, so that we can balance the batch size during training phase.

Note that, there are some overlapping entity spans in the given data set, therefore the flat-NER method, like classical BERT-CRF model, could not perform well on this data set. In detail, nested spans exist in 172 pieces, and most of them are in event triggers. For example, in Doc.13334, there are overlapping argument spans in the second trigger.

Table 1. Statistics of each event type and its role in the data set

SoftHardwareFault	Total	Subject	State	Object	Owner
	19,129	10,693	6,477	1,836	113
SettingFault	Total	Setting	State	Owner	Reference
	5,104	2,366	1,917	789	29
IndexFault	Total	Index	State	Owner	
	4,600	4,542	35	19	
Check	Total	Object	Owner	Object	
	2,799	2,772	13	14	
SetMachine	Total	Object	FinalState	InitialState	Network
	2,052	1,618	302	102	21
Operate	Total	Object	Owner		
	1,589	1,357	227		
CollectData	Total	Data	Source		
	125	108	17		
ExternalFault	Total	State			
	1	1			

4.2 Implementation

We utilized several base models pre-trained on large scale Chinese corpus in both stage and the finetuned on all the weights including the layers of base models. For Stage-1, we set the learning rate to 1×10^{-5} using AdamW optimizer, the batch size is set to 4 and the model is trained for 15 epochs. For Stage-2, we set the learning rate to 3×10^{-5} using AdamW optimizer, the batch size is set to 4 and the model is trained for 20 epochs. For each stage, we trained 3 models for every chosen base models and use voting strategy to ensemble the results of these models.

All programs are implemented by PyTorch framework, and trained on nvidia Tesla V100 GPU.

For data set, we split the provided labelled data into train set and validation set randomly as the ratio of 95:5. All models are trained on the split train set and evaluated on the split evaluation set.

4.3 Competition Result

Benefited from the biaffine attention mechanism and strategies, we got an' F1-score of 0.8033 for the final submission on the final test set, which is the first place in this competition. Besides, we got an F1-score of 0.8975 in the validation set, also the first place in leaderboard.

4.4 Ablation Study

We conduct the ablation study on our approach and strategies to prove their improvements for each stage. Details are as the Table 2 shows. Note that

F1-scores of Stage-1 are calculated on our split validation set, and F1-scores of Stage-2 are calculated by the competition platform in the Test Phase.

Table 2. Ablation study result

Stage	Model methods	F1-score
Stage-1	Baseline	0.8161
	+ biaffine attention	0.8288
	+ uniform multi-label cross-entropy	0.8293
	+ adversarial learning	0.8313
	+ model ensemble	**0.8342**
Stage-2	Baseline	0.7805
	+ biaffine attention	0.7923
	+ uniform multi-label cross-entropy	0.7942
	+ adversarial learning	0.8006
	+ model ensemble	**0.8033**

The baseline model is construct as original BERT model, normal pointer networks and normal cross-entropy loss and trained without adversarial learning. All experiments include data processing strategies. The experiment result shows that biaffine attention mechanism performs better than the classic pointer networks obviously because of the global view of the head and the tail pointer. And by using the uniform multi-label cross-entropy as loss function to train models, there's a bit of improvements that the ordinary one. Adversarial learning helps the robustness of the trained model but slow down the training speed. Obviously, we get a large improvement by model ensemble since we trained a series of models based on 3 large BERT-like models and voted the predictions by a heuristic strategy.

5   Conclusion

The CCKS 2021 Communication Field Domain Event Extraction Task is a text extraction competition in a professional corpus. We purposed a solution that combine the state-of-the-art BERT-like base models pre-trained on Chinese corpus and the biaffine attention mechanism to form a two-stage model. And this model outperforms on the competition data set with an F1-score of 0.8033 as the first place ranking.

In future, we're looking forward to the improved biaffine attention of pointer networks and global pointer networks for a better NER performance. And we'll explore the approach like single-stage model to outperform current two-stage solution.

References

1. Sultana, S., Cavaletto, L.A., Bosu, A.: Identifying the prevalence of gender biases among the computing organizations. arXiv preprint arXiv:2107.00212 (2021)
2. Liu, J., et al.: Event extraction as machine reading comprehension. In: Proceedings of the 2020 Conference on Empirical Methods in Natural Language Processing (2020)
3. Chen, Y., et al.: Automatically labeled data generation for large scale event extraction. In: Proceedings of the 55th Annual Meeting of the Association for Computational Linguistics (2017)
4. Kim, J.-T., Moldovan, D.I.: Acquisition of linguistic patterns for knowledge-based information extraction. IEEE Trans. Knowl. Data Eng. **7**(5), 713–724 (1995)
5. Riloff, E., Shoen, J.: Automatically acquiring conceptual patterns without an annotated corpus. In: Third Workshop on Very Large Corpora (1995)
6. Jiang, J.: A method of obtaining event information extraction mode. Comput. Eng. (2005)
7. Sha, L., et al.: Jointly extracting event triggers and arguments by dependency-bridge RNN and tensor-based argument interaction. In: Thirty-Second AAAI Conference on Artificial Intelligence (2018)
8. Huang, L., et al.: Zero-shot transfer learning for event extraction (2017)
9. Yang, S., et al.: Exploring pre-trained language models for event extraction and generation. In: Proceedings of the 57th Annual Meeting of the Association for Computational Linguistics (2019)
10. Zheng, S., et al.: Doc2EDAG: an end-to-end document-level framework for Chinese financial event extraction. arXiv preprint arXiv:1904.07535 (2019)
11. He, R.F., Duan, S.Y.: Joint Chinese event extraction based multi-task learning. J. Softw. **30**(4), 1015 (2019)
12. Jiang, M., et al.: A study of machine-learning-based approaches to extract clinical entities and their assertions from discharge summaries. J. Am. Med. Inform. Assoc. **18**(5), 601–606 (2011)
13. Nguyen, T.H., Cho, K., Grishman, R.: Joint event extraction via recurrent neural networks. In: Proceedings of the 2016 Conference of the North American Chapter of the Association for Computational Linguistics: Human Language Technologies (2016)
14. Wang, R., Zhou, D., He, Y.: Open event extraction from online text using a generative adversarial network. arXiv preprint arXiv:1908.09246 (2019)
15. Zhang, J., et al.: Extracting entities and events as a single task using a transition-based neural model. In: IJCAI (2019)
16. Dozat, T., Manning, C.D.: Deep biaffine attention for neural dependency parsing. arXiv preprint arXiv:1611.01734 (2016)
17. Sheng, J., et al.: A joint learning framework for the CCKS-2020 financial event extraction task. Data Intell. **3**(3), 444–459 (2021)
18. Yu, J., Bohnet, B., Poesio, M.: Named entity recognition as dependency parsing. arXiv preprint arXiv:2005.07150 (2020)
19. Su, J.: Apply softmax cross-entropy loss function to multi-label classification. https://kexue.fm/archives/7359. Accessed 10 Sept 2021

Method Description for CCKS 2021 Task 3: A Classification Approach of Scholar Structured Information Extraction from HTML Web Pages

Haishun Nan[✉] and Wanshun Wei[✉]

Ping An Puhui Enterprise Management Co. Ltd., Shenzhen, China
nanhaishun@hit.edu.cn

Abstract. Information extractions is a fundamental mission when constructing a scholar profile with the rapid development of AI and big data, especially in the searching task and recommendation system. Therefore, extracting, tagging and statistical analysis the precision facts of experts and scholar can be applied in academic searching. In this paper, a structured information extraction and match approach for structured scholar portrait from HTML web pages based on classification models is demonstrated in detail.

Keywords: Information extraction · Semantic match · Classification models

1 Introduction

With the fast increasing of the information, how to extract structured information from lots of HTML web pages have become an important approach to acquiring knowledge. In the academic field, the aim of a scholar profile is to extract precise information from amount of HTML web pages and can be applied in academic searching, scientific serving, talent scouts and so on. Therefore, the rapid development technology of constructing a scholar profile can promote the progress of the academic intelligence system. However, amounts of HTML web pages always have difference structures and corresponding extraction rules. The method based on statistical rules greatly discount the extraction efficiency. Therefore, it is very important to introduce effective structured extraction information when constructing scholar profiles. CCKS 2021 Task 3, aims to extract structured information such as scholar's homepages, gender, emails, titles, language from HTML web pages.

2 Task Description

The task input are scholar's names, organizations and corresponding searching results where each scholar has 2 pages. And raw HTML format files which is corresponded to

---

H. Nan and W. Wei—These authors contributed equally to this work and should be considered co-first authors

© Springer Nature Singapore Pte Ltd. 2022
B. Qin et al. (Eds.): CCKS 2021, CCIS 1553, pp. 11–17, 2022.
https://doi.org/10.1007/978-981-19-0713-5_2

```
<html>
    <body>
        <td valign="TOP" class="main">
        <h2> Geoffrey E. Hinton</h2>
         </td>


        ...


        <td>
            <b>
                <a href="http://www.toronto.edu/">University of Toronto</a>
            </b>
        </td>
        ...
        ...
    </body>
</html>
```

Fig. 1. Html-format example

searching results is also given. The required output is a Json-format content including scholar's homepages, gender, emails, titles, language. The sample formats of HTML files are described in Fig. 1 and the corresponding output results are illustrated in Fig. 2.

```
{
    "id": "53f31871dabfae9a84425de7",
    "name": "Xiao Ming",
    "org": "University of CCC",
    "homepage":['http://****.edu/~bose/', 'https://sites.google.com/view/***'],
    "email":["*****@edu.cn","*****@163.com"],
    "title": "Professor(教授)",
    "gender": "male",
    "lang": "chinese",
    "avatar": "http://*****.edu/images/***.jpg"
}
```

Fig. 2. Json-format Result

3 Relevant Work

There are two traditional methods for this task. One is Statistical-Based extraction, which applied the matching method on HTML files based on rules, such as wrapper. Due to different kinds of HTML web pages, extracting structured information based on corresponding rules. The other is supervised learning algorithm based on the labeled data. However, the two methods still exist a common weakness, that is inefficiency and low generalization performance. The two methods can only applied rule-based HTML web pages or labeled HTML web pages. It is too expensive due to the requirement of extensive manual processing when processing hundreds of HTML web pages. In this paper, combined with a strategy of filter data, a classification-based method of structured information extraction from HTML web pages is presented. The extraction task is split into five classification tasks.

4   Structured Information Extraction and Matching

In this paper, we put forward a classification-based method of scholar structured information extraction and has a fairly accuracy. In addition, the methods also satisfy certain requirements for structured information extraction.

4.1   Task Decomposition and Filter Strategy for Data

The aim of CCKS 2021 Task 3 is to extract information from amounts of HTML web pages, considering the drawbacks of statistical-based methods, a string matching approach is adopted for the preprocessing of data and all the scholar's homepages, gender, emails, titles, language are extracted. By analyzing the extracted information, the task is split into five classification tasks. Due to the extraction ways of all the scholar's homepages, gender, emails, titles, language, the distributing of extracted sample for classification tasks is unbalanced. Therefore, different filter strategies for data are applied for different classification tasks.

4.2   Three Classifications Tasks for Title, Language an Gender

Firstly, the extractions of scholar's title, language and gender are split into three classifications. When preprocessing the data, for each scholar, a concat operation is used on the texts in first five HTML web pages of the first searching pages. The inputs of classification models are the concat text combined with the scholar's name and organizations. The corresponding labels are constructed by the extracted information categories. Take the scholar's gender as example, the concat text is denoted as 'candidate_text', the sample formats of model inputs is the concat text of scholar's name, organization and candidate text. The corresponding label dict is {'':3,'female':2,'male':0,'no_records':1,'unknown':4}。The comparison of different pretrained models for three classification tasks is displayed in Table 1, where the best_val_score, the best_epoch are respectively average loss and average epoch for three classification tasks.

4.3   Emails Tasks

Secondly, the classification task is to extract scholar's email. In the preprocessing of data, the concat texts are constructed as for scholar's title, language and gender. Then

Table 1. Comparison of different pretrained models for three classifications tasks.

Name	Best_val_loss	Best_epoch
Bert-base-cased	1.481473565	1.4
Bert-base-multilingual-cased	1.487034678	1.4
Roberta-base	1.488482666	1.8
textattack/Roberta-base-MNLI	1.491999459	1.6
Bert-base-uncased	1.498036551	1.4
Bert-base-multilingual-uncased	1.514813352	1.4
Cardiffnlp/twitter-roberta-base-sentiment	1.554109287	2
Google/Electra-base-discriminator	1.579833895	2.5
Camembert-base	1.772359669	3.75

the candidate emails are extracted from the concat texts. By using he candidate emails combined with true scholar's email, the negative samples and positive samples can be obtained for binary classification. When the candidate email is the true scholar's email, the corresponding sample is a positive sample. Conversely, when the candidate email is not the true scholar's email, the corresponding sample is a negative sample. The sample formats of model inputs include the scholar's candidate email, name, organization and candidate text. By monitoring the recall rate, the comparison of different pretrained models for email classification tasks is displayed in Table 2, where the best_val_score, the best_epoch are respectively loss and the best epoch for the email classification tasks.

Table 2. Comparison of different pretrained models for emails tasks.

Name	Best_val_loss	Best_epoch
Albert-base-v2	0.057714213	2
Albert-base-v1	0.048560675	4
Bert-base-multilingual-uncased	0.047498904	1
Roberta-base	0.042537935	4
Bert-base-cased	0.053411789	1
Google/Electra-base-discriminator	0.130018353	7
Bert-base-uncased	0.055880055	1
Bert-base-multilingual-cased	0.044085234	0

4.4 Homepages Tasks

Thirdly, similar to email task, the homepages extraction can be taken as a binary classification task. The concat texts are constructed as the email tasks. And the candidate homepages are extract from the first ten texts in HTML web pages from the first searching page. Combined with true scholar's homepages and candidate homepages, the negative samples and positive samples can be obtained for binary classification. When the candidate homepage is the true scholar's homepage, the corresponding sample is a positive sample, while when the candidate homepage is not the true scholar's homepage, the corresponding sample is a negative sample. The sample formats of model inputs include the sequence numbers of homepage, candidate homepages, scholar's name, organization and concat text. By monitoring the recall rate, the comparison of different pretrained models for homepage classification task is displayed in Table 3, where the best_val_score, the best_epoch are respectively loss and the best epoch for the homepage classification tasks.

Table 3. Comparison of different pretrained models for homepages tasks.

Name	Best_val_loss	Best_epoch
Google/Electra-base-discriminator	0.083208777	2
Roberta-base	0.082423829	1
Bert-base-cased	0.081171595	1
Bert-base-uncased	0.08076033	1
Albert-base-v1	0.076926991	4
Albert-base-v2	0.083409116	3
Bert-base-multilingual-uncased	0.080322191	1
Bert-base-multilingual-cased	0.078788586	1

4.5   Others

In this paper, the structured information extraction task is split into five classification tasks, where the three of them are multiple classifications and the others are binary classifications. At the meantime, a filter strategy of data is applied in these classification tasks, to reduce the imbalance impact on the performance of models. In addition, the comparison of different pretrained models for five classification tasks are made, where the pretrained models include Bert-base-uncased [1], Roberta [2], Albert [3], Bert-base-multilingual-cased[1,2] and Electra-base-discriminator [4]. In the final submit results, Bert-base-multilingual-cased pretrained models is chosen for five classification tasks due to the experiments results in Sect. 4.2–4.4. It is noticed that in the email task and homepages task, the final results of the two tasks are the top1 results. To get the top1 results, we first sorted probabilities in descending order, and choose the top1 probabilities that is greater than 0.48.

---

[1] https://huggingface.co/bert-base-multilingual-cased.

[2] Bert-base-multilingual-cased.

Bert-base-multilingual-cased is a 12-layer transformer with token embeddings of size 768, trained by Google on the Wikipedia of 104 languages, including Chinese Hindi and English (Table 4).

Table 4. Bert-base-multilingual-cased Hyperparameters.

Hyperparameter	Value
Attention_probs_dropout_prob	0.1
Directionality	bidi
Hidden_act	gelu
Hidden_dropout_prob	0.1
Hidden_size	768
Layer_norm_eps	1E-12
Max_position_embeddings	512
Num_attention_heads	12
Num_hidden_layers	12
Pooler_fc_size	768
Pooler_num_attention_heads	12
Pooler_num_fc_layers	3
Pooler_size_per_head	128
Pooler_type	first_token_transform
Vocab_size	119547

5   Conclusions

This paper has put forward a classification methods to extract scholar structured information from HTML web pages. A pretrained models and filter strategy of data is adopted, the information extraction task is split into five classification tasks. This system also achieved 0.70982 in score of the CCKS2021 task 3 evaluation. This design finally ranked No. 4 among all teams for the overall task 3. This design finally ranked No. 4 among all teams for the overall task 3. Such results also have proved the effectiveness of our approach.

References

1. Devlin, J., Chang, M.W., Lee, K., Toutanova, K.: Bert: Pre-training of deep bidirectional transformers for language understanding. arXiv preprint arXiv:1810.04805. 6 (2018)
2. Liu, Y., et al.: RoBERTa: A Robustly Optimized BERT Pretraining Approach

3. Lan, Z., Chen, M., Goodman, S., Gimpel, K., Sharma, P., Soricut, R.: ALBERT: A Lite BERT for Self-supervised Learning of Language Representations
4. Clark, K., Luong, M.T., Le, Q.V., Manning, C.D.: ELECTRA: Pre-training Text Encoders as Discriminators Rather Than Generators

A Dual-Classifier Model for General Fine-Grained Event Detection Task

Yiming Hei[1], Qian Li[2], Caibo Zhou[3], Rui Sun[2], Jinglin Yang[4,5,6],
Jiawei Sheng[4,5], Shu Guo[6], and Lihong Wang[6(✉)]

[1] School of Cyber Science and Technology, Beihang University, Beijing, China
black@buaa.edu.cn
[2] School of Computer Science, Beihang University, Beijing, China
[3] School of Economics and Management, Beihang University, Beijing, China
[4] Institute of Information Engineering, Chinese Academy of Sciences, Beijing, China
shengjiawei@iie.ac.cn
[5] School of Cyber Security, University of Chinese Academy of Sciences,
Beijing, China
[6] National Computer Network Emergency Response Technical Team/Coordination
Center of China, Beijing, China
guoshu@cert.org.cn, wlh@isc.org.cn

Abstract. This paper presents a winning solution for the CCKS-2021 general fine-grained event detection task whose goal is to identify event triggers and the corresponding event types from the MAssive eVENt detection dataset (MAVEN). In this task, we focus on two challenging problems in MAVEN: event identification and event confusion. The former problem is that it is hard to determine whether the current trigger word triggers an event. The latter problem means that some events are prone to category confusion. To solve the event identification issue, we propose a dual-classifier event detection model, which combines event identification and event classification to enhance the ability to judge the existence of events. In addition, to solve the problem of event confusion, we introduce adversarial training strategies to enhance the robustness of event category boundaries. The approach achieves an F1-score of 0.7058, ranking the first place in the competition.

Keywords: Event detection · Fine-grained event · Event identification · CCKS-2021 competition

1 Introduction

The CCKS-2021 Massive General Domain Fine-grained Event Detection Challenge[1] aims at identifying general events of particular type from massive plain text. Specifically, the competition requires to locate the event triggers (i.e., the keywords or phrases that express the occurrence of the event most clearly) from a given text, and then classify these triggers into their corresponding event types.

---

[1] https://www.biendata.xyz/competition/ccks_2021_maven/.

© Springer Nature Singapore Pte Ltd. 2022
B. Qin et al. (Eds.): CCKS 2021, CCIS 1553, pp. 18–27, 2022.
https://doi.org/10.1007/978-981-19-0713-5_3

As the first step of event extraction, Event Detection has become a cornerstone task for event knowledge acquisition and event knowledge graph construction.

Aside from general Event detection task, we introduce the specific definition in this competition as follows. Given an event mention (i.e., a sentence with potential event occurrence), the competition further provides several candidate triggers with external annotation. The goal is to select the true triggers from the candidate triggers, and then classify these triggers into 168 fine-grained event types, such as Coming_to_be and Catastrophe event type. Those candidate triggers that don't trigger any events are termed as negative triggers. For example, given an event mention "The 2005 Lake Tanganyika earthquake occurred at on 5 December with a moment magnitude of 6.8.", there exists a candidate trigger list {"Lake", "earthquake", "occurred"}. We would like to recognize "occurred" as a trigger of event type Coming_to_be, "earthquake" as a trigger of event type Catastrophe, and the negative trigger "Lake", which relates to a newly defined event: None (denotes that it doesn't trigger any event).

In this task, we mainly focus on two challenging problems in MAVEN:

(i) Event identification problem, which means that it's hard to judge whether the current trigger triggers a event. Specifically, we make statistics on MAVEN and find that the number of negative triggers is about 4 times than that of positive triggers. And the events corresponding to the positive triggers are further divided into 168 predefined categories. This means that the None event has a clear quantitative advantage over the other 168 predefined events. In this case, the predefined event can easily be confused with the None event, causing difficulties in event identification.

(ii) Event confusion problem, which means that the given event types are easily confused. There are complex relationships among 168 fine-grained event types in this task, such as hierarchical relationship and event semantic similarity. Take the event Military_operation as an example, it is not only the child event of Violence, but also the parent event of Hostile_encounter. In addition, semantically similar events can also be easily found in 168 event types, such as Assistance and Supporting, Destroying and Damaging, Commerce_pay and Commerce_sell. Through experimental testing, it is hard to distinguish the events with hierarchical relationships (such as parent-child relationships) or similar semantics [12]. Simply put, it means that the boundaries between some event categories are not obvious.

To address the challenges mentioned above, we develop a corresponding event detection approach, aiming at improving the event detection ability for fine-grained events. Concretely, for event identification problem, we design a dual classifier model, which effectively combines the information of whether the event exists with the event classification. This model improves the ability to identify events and further improves the event classification performance. For event confusion problem, we introduce adversarial training strategies to enhance the robustness of event category boundaries. Our approach achieves a F1-score of 0.7058 and ranks first in the CCKS-2021 massive general domain fine-grained event detection challenge competition.

2   Related Work

DMCNN [1] is the first work on event detection via Convolutional Neural Network (CNN) model, which automatically learns effective feature representations from pre-trained word embeddings, position embeddings as well as entity type embeddings to reduce the error propagation. Almost at the same time, the Recurrent Neural Network (RNN)-based model [5] is applied to detect the event nuggets (cross-word trigger word) in the event detection task. The representation learning approaches used in the above scheme are difficult to capture long distance dependencies in event mentions and thus achieves poor performance. To tackle this issue, attention mechanism is introduced into event detection. Chen et al. [2] proposes an event detection framework which can automatically extract and dynamically integrate sentence-level and document-level information and collectively detect multiple events in one sentence. A gated multi-level attention is devised to automatically extract and dynamically integrate contextual information. Liu et al. [10] proposes to use the annotated argument information explicitly by a supervised attention based Event detection model, and Zhao et al. [15] designs a hierarchical and supervised attention based and document embedding enhanced Bi-RNN method for event detection. It explores different strategies to construct gold word and sentence-level attentions to focus on event information. Besides, [14] further takes BERT [4] as the encoder to learn better representations for event mentions. In order to further leverage the correlation between events, the researchers introduce the graph model. [13] designs a model for modeling multi-order representations via Graph Attention Network (GAT) [11] and employs an attention aggregation mechanism to better capture dependency contextual information for event detection. [3] proposes an Event detection model named Edge-Enhanced Graph Convolutional Networks [8], which introduces the typed dependency label information into the graph modeling process, and learns to update the relation representations in a context-dependent manner.

In addition to the above-mentioned conventional methods, the researchers also uses adversarial training [7], machine reading comprehension [9] to improve the performance of the Event detection model, and achieves good results.

3   Our Approach

Task Description
Generally speaking, event detection consists of two subtasks: identifying trigger words (trigger identification) and classifying them into the correct event types (event classification). Similar to existing works, we integrate the above two subtasks into a (N + 1)-classification task (N denotes the number of pre-defined event types) by introducing a None class, indicating non-event. In particular, the trigger word corresponding to the None event is defined as negative trigger. Formally, Let $Text = [w_1, w_2, ..., w_n]$ be a sentence of length n of some event trigger candidates, where w_c ($1 \leq c \leq n$) is the current candidate word for event detection. Our goal is to determine the event type y for the candidate w_c.

3.1 Overview

Our overall approach can be divided into three parts: data pre-processing module, dual-classifier event detection model, and model ensemble module. In the data preprocess part, we integrated feature that is helpful for event detection. In the detection model part, based on the selected features, we built a dual classifier module to incorporate the event identification information into the multi-classification model and take advantage of adversarial training to enhance the robustness of event category boundaries. In the model ensemble module, we introduced a multi-model result fusion module further improve the performance.

3.2 Data Pre-processing

In the data pre-processing module, we integrate information that is helpful for event detection, including trigger part of speech (POS) and article title. In addition, we also enhance the specificity of the original text under a specific trigger word by prefixing each trigger word in the head of the original text.

Input Feature Selection

1. Trigger words. Through data analysis, we found a single-sentence multi-event case in the competition corpus, i.e., there are multiple candidate trigger words in a single sentence, and each trigger word triggers an event category (for the non-event category, we define its category as None). In this case, to enable the model to detect the possible existence of multiple event types from a single sentence, we splice the trigger words into the head of the text. In this way, we enhance the specificity of the corpus under different trigger words, which is equivalent to implicitly tell the model that the trigger word needed to focus on is at the head of the text.
2. Part-of-Speech of Trigger word. We also find that there are more obvious differences in Part-of-Speech (POS) features between real trigger words and negative sample trigger words. That is, real trigger words tend to be verbs, while negative triggers are mostly nouns. Therefore, we not only splice the trigger words in the sentence head but also add the lexical labels of the trigger words using the NLTK tool.
3. Title. Since the event mentions are chosen from documents, the event categories under the same document tend to have some correlation because they share the topic of the source document. In order to incorporate such semantic information of documents, we also splice the title of the document after the original text. By this means, the semantic information of the original corpus is enhanced on the one hand, and the correlation of the corpus under the same document is improved. On the other hand, we implicitly enhancing the correlation between events within the same document.

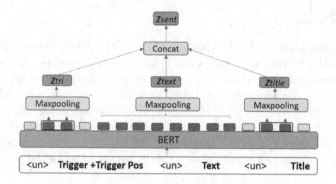

Fig. 1. The data pre-processing module.

3.3 Dual-Classifier Event Detection Model

As shown in Fig. 1, after adding the above additional features to the original text, we input the newly obtained text corpus into the BERT [4] model to obtain a generic text feature representation

$$z = BERT(< UN >, w_c, POS(w_c), < UN >, Text, < UN >, Title), \quad (1)$$

where "$< UN >$" denotes the special symbol in BERT. Then, we do Max Pooling on the output feature vectors of Trigger + Trigger Pos (z_{tri}), Text (z_{text}), and Title (z_{title}) respectively, and concat all the pooled results to get the final feature vector

$$z_{sent} = Maxpooling(z_{tri})||Maxpooling(z_{text})||Maxpooling(z_{title}). \quad (2)$$

Next, we put the z_{sent} to our classification model (see Fig. 2) which consists of two classifiers: classifier A and classifier B. The input part of both classifiers is vector z_{sent}. Among them, the output of classifier A is a value between 0 and 1, which is used to measure the probability that the current trigger word triggers a **non-None** event. The output of classifier B is a vector of dimension N, corresponding to N **non-None** event types.

The running process of the entire dual classifier model is as follows: Given a vector z_{sent}, we input it into two classifiers at the same time to get the output results h_A and h_B through

$$h_A = \sigma(W_A \cdot z_{sent} + b_A), \quad (3)$$

$$h_B = \sigma(W_B \cdot z_{sent} + b_B), \quad (4)$$

where σ is the sigmoid activation function, W_A, b_A and W_B, b_B are learnable parameters of the two classifiers respectively. Then, we multiply h_A by each element in h_B to get the N-dimensional event probability distribution

$$p(c_N, ..., c_2, c_1 | z_{sent}) = h_A \odot h_B \quad (5)$$

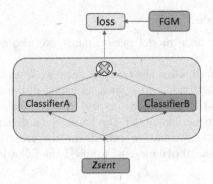

Fig. 2. The frame of two-classification event detection.

of the current trigger W_c, where $\odot$ defines the operation for the dot product of each value in h_B and h_A. Finally, according to the probability distribution $p(c_N, ..., c_2, c_1|z_{sent})$ and the corresponding true label $T = [t_N, ..., t_2, t_1]$, we use the BCE loss function to calculate the training loss:

$$Loss = \sum_{n=1}^{N} t_n \cdot log p(c_n|z_{sent}) + (1 - t_n) \cdot log(1 - p(c_n|z_{sent})). \tag{6}$$

In this way, we use two classifiers to distinguish None from other events, alleviating the problem of data imbalance.

Adversarial Training
The Fast Gradient Sign Method [6] (FGSM) was used to construct some adversarial samples to be added to the original dataset during training to enhance the robustness of the model to the adversarial samples. The principle of this method to generate adversarial samples is to induce the network to misclassify the generated samples by adding increments in the gradient direction. Formally, the adversarial examples z'_{sent} can be calculated with

$$z'_{sent} = z_{sent} + \epsilon \cdot sign(\nabla Loss(z_{sent}, \Theta)), \tag{7}$$

where ϵ is a weight parameter, *sign* is a symbolic function, Θ represents the model parameters. We add the adversarial training algorithm when calculating the model loss to further improve the robustness of our model.

Post-process
In the Post-process module, we define a threshold *thred*. And we stipulate that if the probability value of all events in $p(c_N, ..., c_2, c_1|z_{sent})$ is lower than *thred*, the model determines that the event type is None. Otherwise, we take the event corresponding to the largest probability in $p(c_N, ..., c_2, c_1|z_{sent})$ as the predicted event.

3.4 Model Ensemble

In order to further enhance model performance, we also adopt a multi-model ensemble module.

For different ways of dividing the training data, we train the model under four different data set construction ratios such as using all data for training, 5-fold cross-validation, 10-fold cross-validation, and 20-fold cross-validation. Also, we set different trigger thresholds under the same data division ratio and saved the model under multiple iteration rounds in the training process. For the results obtained from the above models, we used the following two model fusion methods.

Hierarchical Ensemble Method: In considering the model fusion process, we consider a layer-by-layer fusion, i.e., constructing a similar relationship tree of the models. When adjusting the hyperparameters of a layer in the integrated model, the fusion of its next layer can be fixed as simple voting, and the parameters are adjusted and then iterated as a whole for the fusion parameters of its further layer. In this process, the number of super parameters to be adjusted in a single model is significantly compressed. Fast iterative optimization can be performed with a limited number of tuned parameters, ensuring that better results can be achieved with the use of using a small number of model results.

Voting Ensemble Method: In order to further reduce the hyperparameters, with sufficient computational resources, we performed model integration for all 150 models obtained from training through a simple minority-majority voting strategy.

Method Comparison: We found that the Voting Ensemble method can effectively improve the generalization ability of the models and has a significant effect on the performance improvement (the best result of the competition list was achieved). However, compared with Voting Ensemble method, Hierarchical Ensemble method can achieve better results when the number of models is small, which adapts to the situation of low computing resources.

4 Experiment

This section introduces the dataset provided in the competition, and conducts experiments to evaluate the model.

4.1 Dataset

The dataset used in the CCKS-2021 is a MAssive eVENt detection dataset (MAVEN) [12]. It totally contains 4480 Wikipedia documents, 49873 sentences, and 168 event types and is split into training, development, and test sets. For training set, there are 2913 documents in it. Each document contains title, sentences, events, triggers for each event and negative triggers. The development and test sets consist of 710 and 857 documents, respectively. There is only the title, sentences and the trigger candidates in the two sets. More details for these subsets are listed in Table 1.

Table 1. The statistics of the subsets in the competition

Subset	Document	Sentence	Event triggers	Negative triggers	Trigger candidates
Train	2913	32431	77993	323992	–
Dev	710	8042	–	–	98603
Test	857	9400	–	–	115405

4.2 Hyper-parameters

Based on the huggingface framework, we treat the BERT model bert-base-uncased with 12 layers and 768 hidden size as our pre-trained language model. For the dual-classifier model, the initial learning rate for Adam is set to 5e-5, the batch size is set to 42, the maximum sequence length of tokens is 128, the power exponent of the probability value λ is 5, the *thred* is 0.83. All the hyperparameters are tuned by grid-search.

4.3 Main Result

Table 2 shows the performance on test data: based on the optimal hyperparameters given above, the performance of the single model reaches a 0.7031 F1-score. We think that the reasons for this performance are as follows: 1. We fully excavated and utilized the key feature information hidden in the data set. 2. We discovered the impact of event identification on event detection and effectively integrated this information into the model. 3. Through adversarial training, we enhance the robustness of the event boundary. The final F1 value is improved by 0.17% and 0.27%, respectively, by designing hierarchical ensemble and voting ensemble in Sect. 3.4 based on a re-optimal single model. The result of the multi-model ensemble is the highest score in the competition.

4.4 Ablation Study

We conduct an ablation study on our single event detection model, where the results are shown in Table 3. Our model has the highest values in F1-score and Precision, and the results show that our model can better solve generic event detection problem. After the dual-classification structure is removed, the

Table 2. The performance of our proposed model.

Model	P	R	F1
Single model	0.6981	0.7081	0.7031
Hierarchical ensemble	0.7016	0.7079	0.7048
Voting ensemble	0.6971	0.7145	0.7058

Table 3. Ablation study on test data.

Model	P	R	F1
Single model	0.6981	0.7081	0.7031
w/o Dual-classification structure	0.6848	0.6962	0.6904
w/o Adversarial Training	0.6549	0.7198	0.6858

F1 value of the model decreases by 1.03%, which indicates that the dual-classification structure have stronger event identification ability, thus it can classify events more accurately. In addition, When the adversarial training module is removed, the F1 value decreases by 2.4%, which indicates that adversarial training module makes the boundary of event category more robust, which is important to the performance of fine-grained multi-event classification. All the results demonstrate the effectiveness of each component in the model and Event detection task.

5   Conclusion

In this paper, we propose a fine-grained event detection method for general domain based on a joint classification framework. It can effectively mine the information in event mentions and improve the performance of the model in distinguishing whether events exist or not and enhance the robustness of event boundaries. The experimental results show that the approach achieves remarkable performance, and it won the first place in the CCKS-2021 massive general domain fine-grained event detection challenge competition.

Acknowledgement. This work is supported by the National Natural Science Foundation of China (No. 61772151, No. 62106059, No. U21B2021, No.61932014, No. 61972018).

References

1. Chen, Y., Xu, L., Liu, K., Zeng, D., Zhao, J.: Event extraction via dynamic multi-pooling convolutional neural networks. In: Proceedings of the 53rd Annual Meeting of the Association for Computational Linguistics and the 7th International Joint Conference on Natural Language Processing of the Asian Federation of Natural Language Processing, pp. 167–176 (2015)
2. Chen, Y., Yang, H., Liu, K., Zhao, J., Jia, Y.: Collective event detection via a hierarchical and bias tagging networks with gated multi-level attention mechanisms. In: Proceedings of the 2018 Conference on Empirical Methods in Natural Language Processing, pp. 1267–1276. Association for Computational Linguistics (2018)
3. Cui, S., Yu, B., Liu, T., Zhang, Z., Wang, X., Shi, J.: Edge-enhanced graph convolution networks for event detection with syntactic relation. In: Findings of the Association for Computational Linguistics, pp. 2329–2339. Association for Computational Linguistics (2020)

4. Devlin, J., Chang, M., Lee, K., Toutanova, K.: BERT: pre-training of deep bidirectional transformers for language understanding. In: Proceedings of the 2019 Conference of the North American Chapter of the Association for Computational Linguistics, pp. 4171–4186. Association for Computational Linguistics (2019)
5. Ghaeini, R., Fern, X.Z., Huang, L., Tadepalli, P.: Event nugget detection with forward-backward recurrent neural networks. CoRR arXiv:1802.05672 (2018)
6. Goodfellow, I.J., Shlens, J., Szegedy, C.: Explaining and harnessing adversarial examples. In: 3rd International Conference on Learning Representations, ICLR 2015, Conference Track Proceedings, San Diego, CA, USA, 7–9 May 2015 (2015)
7. Hong, Y., Zhou, W., Zhang, J., Zhu, Q., Zhou, G.: Self-regulation: employing a generative adversarial network to improve event detection. In: Proceedings of the 56th Annual Meeting of the Association for Computational Linguistics, pp. 515–526. Association for Computational Linguistics (2018)
8. Kipf, T.N., Welling, M.: Semi-supervised classification with graph convolutional networks. CoRR arXiv:1609.02907 (2016)
9. Liu, J., Chen, Y., Liu, K., Bi, W., Liu, X.: Event extraction as machine reading comprehension. In: Proceedings of the 2020 Conference on Empirical Methods in Natural Language Processing, pp. 1641–1651. Association for Computational Linguistics (2020)
10. Liu, S., Chen, Y., Liu, K., Zhao, J.: Exploiting argument information to improve event detection via supervised attention mechanisms. In: Proceedings of the 55th Annual Meeting of the Association for Computational Linguistics, pp. 1789–1798. Association for Computational Linguistics (2017)
11. Velickovic, P., Cucurull, G., Casanova, A., Romero, A., Liò, P., Bengio, Y.: Graph attention networks. CoRR arXiv:1710.10903 (2017)
12. Wang, X., et al.: MAVEN: a massive general domain event detection dataset. In: Proceedings of the 2020 Conference on Empirical Methods in Natural Language Processing, pp. 1652–1671. Association for Computational Linguistics (2020)
13. Yan, H., Jin, X., Meng, X., Guo, J., Cheng, X.: Event detection with multi-order graph convolution and aggregated attention. In: Proceedings of the 2019 Conference on Empirical Methods in Natural Language Processing and the 9th International Joint Conference on Natural Language Processing, pp. 5765–5769. Association for Computational Linguistics (2019)
14. Yang, S., Feng, D., Qiao, L., Kan, Z., Li, D.: Exploring pre-trained language models for event extraction and generation. In: Proceedings of the 57th Conference of the Association for Computational Linguistics, pp. 5284–5294. Association for Computational Linguistics (2019)
15. Zhao, Y., Jin, X., Wang, Y., Cheng, X.: Document embedding enhanced event detection with hierarchical and supervised attention. In: Proceedings of the 56th Annual Meeting of the Association for Computational Linguistics, pp. 414–419. Association for Computational Linguistics (2018)

A Joint Training Framework Based on Adversarial Perturbation for Video Semantic Tags Classification

Zhenxu Ye[1](✉), Yaoyuan Zhang[2](✉), and Shengming Cao[1](✉)

[1] Tencent, Shenzhen, China
stoneyezhenxu@gmail.com, checkmate.ming@gmail.com
[2] Microsoft, Dublin, Ireland
zhangyao@microsoft.com

Abstract. In this paper, we present a solution of "Knowledge Enhanced Video Semantic Understanding" of 2021 CCKS Track 14th task [1]. We separate video semantic understanding framework into two related tasks, namely the multi-classes video cate classification (VCC) task and the multi-label video tag classification (VTC) task. Meanwhile we propose a joint training framework for VCC task and VTC task based on adversarial perturbations strategy. In the final leaderboard, we achieved 3rd place in the competition. The source code has been at Github (https://github.com/stone-yzx/2021-CCKS-Trace14-3rd-semantic-tag-classification).

Keywords: Video cate classification · Video tag classification · Adversarial perturbations

1 Introduction

The 2021 CCKS Track 14th task of "Knowledge Enhanced Video Semantic Understanding" is held by The CCKS and Baidu. The task aims at multimodal information processing, such as title, RGB frames features, OCR, ASR and embedding them into latent representation for video semantic tags recognition.

1.1 Dataset

There is total 8w official annotated pointwise data, which is composed of 3.7w training data and 2.4w test data (8.3k for test_a set and 1.6w for final test_b).

A video sample of train set contains several fields as shown below:

Title: video title in Chinese
Frame feature: video frame embedding feature extracted from TSN network
ASR: video speech recognition text sequences
OCR: video optical character recognition text sequence
Category: video first and second level category
Tag: video semantic tags

© Springer Nature Singapore Pte Ltd. 2022
B. Qin et al. (Eds.): CCKS 2021, CCIS 1553, pp. 28–33, 2022.
https://doi.org/10.1007/978-981-19-0713-5_4

1.2 Evaluation Metric

In the competition, the evaluation metric is F1-Measure, which can be computed as:

$$P = \frac{\sum_{i \in N}(TG(i) \cap TP(i))}{\sum_{i \in N} TP(i)}$$

$$R = \frac{\sum_{i \in N}(TG(i) \cap TP(i))}{\sum_{i \in N} TG(i)}$$

$$F1 = \frac{2 * P * R}{P + R}$$

Where TG = {t_1, t_2, ..., t_n}, n is the ground truth tags num. TP = {t_1, t_2, ..., t_m}, m is the predict tags num. N is the total video samples.

This competition will output two types of label results (video cate label and video tags label). First, F1 will be calculated separately for each label and then calculate the final F1 final through weighted summation. The calculation formula is as follows:

$$F1_{final} = W_{cate} * F1_{cate} + W_{tags} * F1_{tags}$$

Where the value of W_{cate} and W_{tags} is determined.

2 Methodology

2.1 Framework

Inspired by the Yutube-8M competition [2, 3], we also designed a two-stage framework for this task, as is shown in Fig. 1. The first stage is multimodal feature encoding, and the second stage contains the multimodal feature fusion and classifier projection.

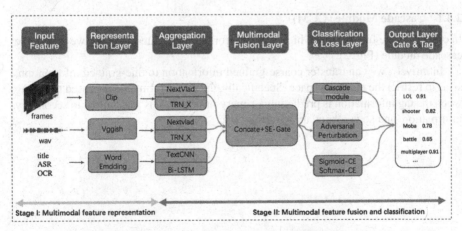

Fig. 1. Proposed framework for VCC task and VTC task

2.2 Multimodal Feature Representation

Through simple feature selection, we mainly use three modals of all supplied features. The feature format and extraction methods are demonstrated as follows.

2.2.1 Rgb Feature

The RGB frame is extracted from video with one frame per second by ffmpeg tools. And then we encode all the frames by Clip model [4].

2.2.2 Audio Feature

The audio file is first transformed into Mel spectrum, and then embedded by Vggish model [5].

2.2.3 Text Feature

The text modal (title & ASR & OCR) is embedded by traditional TextCNN model and Bi-LSTM model respectively. We further concatenate them for further usage. The pre-trained word embedding comes from Tencent AI LAB [6].

2.3 Multimodal Feature Aggregate and Fusion

We use the NeXtVlad model [7] for frame-aggregation of both audio and visual features. As for multimodal feature fusion, we firstly concatenate all the aggregated embedding including title, ASR, OCR, audio and visual frames. The module of SE-GATE is then applied to fuse information among different channels.

2.4 Classification Module Design

2.4.1 Cascade Module (CCM)

In order to make full use of the hierarchical information of cates and tags, we design the cascade module (Fig. 2).

Intuitively, we can transfer coarse-grained information to fine-grained information, so as to restrict the mapping space. Specifically, the cate information is passed to the tag when the tag information is predicting; primary information is transmitted to secondary information, and so is secondary to tertiary one.

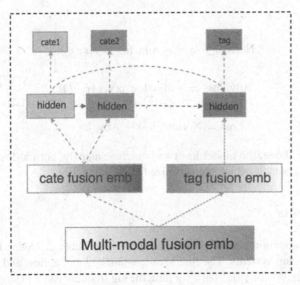

Fig. 2. Cascade module

2.4.2 Adversarial Perturbation Module (APM)

Furthermore, in order to improve the generalization ability of the model and improve the recall of tags, we designed an adversarial perturbation module as shown in Fig. 3.

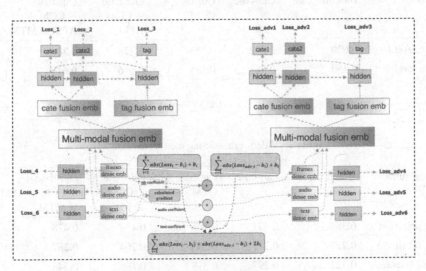

Fig. 3. Adversarial perturbation module

$$\text{Normal\_loss} = -\min \, \log \, p(y|x, \, \theta)$$

$$\text{Adv\_loss} = -\min \, \log \, p(y|x+r, \, \theta)$$

$$\text{Loss} = \text{Normal\_loss} + \text{Adv\_loss}$$

As is shown above, the model has two branches, namely, normal-loss branch and preturbation-loss branch, which are optimized at the same time.

3   Experiments

The results of validation set are shown in Table 1 and Table 2. Notice that we have two-level video cate systems. The first level contains 33 categories, and second level contains 310 ones. As for video tags, we limit the tag frequency to 5 to slightly alleviate the tag sparsity.

Table 1. Video-classify-tag metrics details

Task \ Metrics	Accuracy				
Model	Baseline_cate	Our-base	Our-base + CCM	Our-base + CCM + APM	Our-base + CCM + APM + MTM
Cate level 1	0.620	0.742	0.754	0.778	**0.781**
Cate level 2	0.450	0.583	0.595	0.616	**0.619**

Table 2. Video-sementic-tag metrics details

Metrics\model	Baseline_tag (all tag)	Our-base	Our-base + CCM	Our-base + CCM + APM	Our-base + CCM + APM + MTM
Tag precision	0.586	0.471	0.465	0.474	**0.478**
Tag recall	0.222	0.217	0.236	0.264	**0.267**
Tag F1-scores	0.322	0.297	0.313	0.339	**0.343**

We perform ablation experiments of NeXtVlad module, cascade module (CCM), adversarial perturbation module (APM) and multi-task module(MTM) to see how they affect the original features representation and the model convergence.

In video cate task baseline, the organizer provides an AttentionLSTM-based method [8] (Baseline_cate). While in video-semantic-tag task, they use a transformer-based [9] NER model (Baseline-tag).

In video-sementic-tag task, baseline method is evaluated on all tags and ours is only 1k with a tag frequency limit.

The leaderboard displays the final score of two tasks on test_b set. For video-semantic-tag task, we ensemble the results of baseline-tag model and our-tag model. For video-cate task, only our-cate model is used. In the end, we got a final score of 0.4486.

4 Conclusion

In this paper, we delivered our solution to the 2021 CCKS Track 14. We have designed a multimodal framework for semantic tags classification. The proposed framework has a significant improvement on video tags tasks. However, in this competition, semantic tags are too sparse (50% frequency is less than 5), and the advantage of multimodal framework cannot be fully tapped. In future work, we would try to investigate the method of sparsity alleviation to cope with long-tail tags.

Reference

1. https://www.biendata.xyz/competition/ccks_2021_videounderstanding/finallead.erboard/
2. https://github.com/google/youtube-8m
3. https://github.com/linrongc/youtube-8m
4. Radford, A., Kim, J.W., Hallacy, C., et al.: Learning transferable visual models from natural language supervision. arXiv preprint arXiv:2103.00020 (2021)
5. Hershey, S., Chaudhuri, S., Ellis, D.P.W., et al.: CNN architectures for large-scale audio. Classification. In: 2017 IEEE international conference on acoustics, speech and signal processing (ICASSP). IEEE, pp. 131–135 (2017)
6. https://ai.tencent.com/ailab/nlp/zh/embedding.html
7. Lin, R., Xiao, J., Fan, J.: NeXtVLAD: an efficient neural network to aggregate frame-level features for large-scale video classification. In: Leal-Taixé, L., Roth, S. (eds.) ECCV 2018. LNCS, vol. 11132, pp. 206–218. Springer, Cham (2019). https://doi.org/10.1007/978-3-030-11018-5_19
8. https://github.com/PaddlePaddle/Research/tree/master/KG/DuKEVU_Baseline/paddle-video-classify-tag
9. https://github.com/PaddlePaddle/Research/tree/master/KG/DuKEVU_Baseline/paddle-video-semantic-tag

A Multi-modal System for Video Semantic Understanding

Zhengwei Lv[✉], Tao Lei, Xiao Liang, Zhizhong Shi, and Duoxing Liu

Autohome Inc., Beijing, China
{lvzhengwei,leitao,liangxiao12030,shizhizhong,liuduoxing}@autohome.com.cn

Abstract. This paper proposes a video semantic understanding system based on multi-modal data fusion. The system includes two sub-models, the video classification tag model (VCT) and the video semantic tag model (VST), to generate classification tags and semantic tags for videos respectively. The VCT model uses bidirectional LSTM model and Attention mechanism to integrate the video features, which can effectively improve the model result than other methods. The VST model directly extracts semantic tags from text data with the combined model of ROBERTA and CRF. We implemented the system in the CCKS 2021 Task 14 and achieved an F1 score of 0.5054, ranking second among 187 teams.

Keywords: Multi-modal representation · Semantic understanding · Video

1 Introduction

With the rapid development of video application in the internet, the video semantic understanding has become particularly prominent. In order to promote the research and application of video semantic understanding, Baidu and CCKS (China Conference on Knowledge Graph and Semantic Computing) provided a evaluation task for researchers, named knowledge-enhanced video semantic understanding, at the 15th China Conference on Knowledge Graph and Semantic Computing. This task includes two subtasks: classification tags and semantic tags. It is expected to integrate multi-modal information such as knowledge, language, vision, and speech to generate semantic tags with multiple knowledge dimensions for the video, and then better describe the semantic information of the video.

In image monomodal data scenes for video understanding, these approaches [1,3,14] have achieved good results and have good reference value, which use convolutional neural network and Transformer [20] to model the spatio-temporal sequence of the video. Nowadays, a large amount of video data is multi-modal, including language, vision, voice, etc., and researches on multi-modal understanding of video are constantly appearing [4,9,18,19]. However, the above researches focus on the representation and retrieval of video multi-modality. For the subtask of tag classification, this paper proposes a multi-modal video tag classification model, which uses bidirectional LSTM [5] and attention mechanism [22] to

© Springer Nature Singapore Pte Ltd. 2022
B. Qin et al. (Eds.): CCKS 2021, CCIS 1553, pp. 34–43, 2022.
https://doi.org/10.1007/978-981-19-0713-5_5

get video representation, and uses a feature fusion method in NeXtVLAD [15] to fuse the text features and the aggregated video representation, Achieving good tag classification results.

For the subtask of semantic tag, there are two ways to obtain the semantic tags of the video: generation and extraction. The generation method takes text and image as input, and uses a generative model to obtain semantic tags. This method integrates multi-modal data, so that the tags are not limited to the text, and the tags are more diverse. However, the tag quality is difficult to control with the generation method, resulting in low accuracy. The extraction method takes text data as input, and uses a sequence labeling model to extract corresponding tags from the text. This method extracts tags with high quality, but ignores other modal semantic tags, and the diversity of tags is poor. In order to obtain better system stability and higher tag accuracy, this paper uses the ROBERTA [17] and CRF [10] models to extract the semantic tags of the video from the text data.

This paper constructs a video semantic understanding system based on multi-modal data fusion, which generates semantic tags with multiple knowledge dimensions for video data. The system includes two sub-models, the video classification tag model (VCT) and the video semantic tag model (VST), which generate classification tags and semantic tags for videos respectively. The VCT model first uses the ROBERTA model to obtain the feature representation of the text data, and uses bidirectional LSTM model and Attention mechanism to integrate the video features. Then the model fuses text and video features with a fusion module, and get classification tag with a softmax classifier. The VST model directly combines the ROBERTA and CRF models to extract the semantic tags from the text data. The contributions can be summarized as follows: (1) This paper builds a complete video semantic understanding system with VCT and VST model. (2) We verify the effectiveness of VCT and VST model through experiments.

2 Related Work

In recent years, the researches on the video content understanding have two directions: single-modality and multi-modality. The former focuses on the modeling of image spatio-temporal sequence in video, such as: TSM [14] can achieve the performance of 3D CNN but maintain 2D CNN's complexity, SlowFast [3] proposes a novel two-pathway model, StNet [6] proposes a spatial temporal network architecture for both local and global spatial-temporal modeling in videos. The latter focuses on the representation and fusion of multi-modal data, such as: UniVL [18] proposes a pre-training model for both multi- modal understanding and generation, ActBERT [23] introduces an method for self-supervised learning of joint video-text representations from unlabeled data, HERO [11] encodes multimodal inputs in a hierarchical structure.

Semantic tags extraction belongs to information extraction. Early information extraction mostly used the method of RNN-CRF [8] to obtain the label sequence of the text. With the rapid development of pre-training models such as BERT, ROBERTA and XLNet [2,17,21], the combination of pre-training model and CRF has achieved remarkable results on sequence labeling tasks. Recently, the paper [16] presents a approach to learn NER models in the absence of labelled data through weak supervision, the paper [12] proposes Flat-LAttice Transformer for Chinese NER, which converts the lattice structure into a flat structure consisting of spans.

3   System Description

The system can generate semantic tags with multiple knowledge dimensions for video data, as shown in Fig. 1. First, the video data is preprocessed to obtain text data and frame data, and then the processed data is input into the multi-modal models VCT1 and VCT2 to obtain the first-level and second-level tags of the video. The VCT1 and VCT2 models are VCT models trained for the first-level and second-level tag classification of videos. Finally, input the processed text data into the trained VST model to obtain video semantic tags.

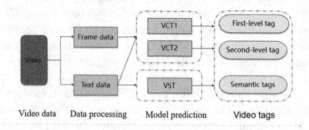

Fig. 1. The video semantic understanding system.

3.1   VCT Model

The VCT model is a multi-modal model that receives the text and image data of the video and predicts the classification tag. The model structure is shown in Fig. 2, which is composed of four parts: text module, image module, feature fusion module and output module.

Text Module. Text data $T = \{x_1, x_2, x_3, \ldots, x_n\}$, x_i represents the i-th Chinese character in the text. Input the text into the pre-trained ROBERTA model and obtain the text vector V, $V = \{v_1, v_2, v_3, \ldots, v_n\}$. We use the following method to get vector H_t the generated by text module:

$$H_t = v_p * V_{cls} \tag{1}$$

where v_p is a trained parameter vector, V_{cls} is the vector of the first index position of the text vector V.

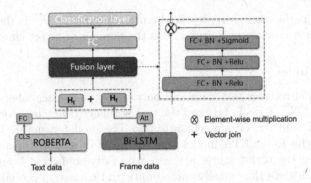

Fig. 2. VCT model, where BN is BatchNormal regularization, and FC is full connection layer. Relu and Sigmoid are activation function.

Image Module. Image data $F = \{f_1, f_2, f_3, ..., f_m\}$, f_i represents the vector of the i-th image extracted from the video. Input the vector sequence F into the bidirectional LSTM model, and get the vector sequence $H = \{h_1, h_2, h_3, ..., h_m\}$, $H \in R^{2*dim \times m}$, where dim is the dimension of the output vector of the LSTM unit, m Is the length of the image sequence. This paper uses the attention mechanism to weight the vector sequence H to obtain the final representation H_f of the image data. The calculation method is as follows:

$$M = tanh(H) \tag{2}$$

$$\alpha = softmax(W^T M) \tag{3}$$

$$\gamma = H\alpha^T \tag{4}$$

$$H_f = tanh(\gamma) \tag{5}$$

where w is a trained parameter vector and w^T is a transpose. The dimension of w, α, γ is 2*dim, m, 2*dim separately.

Feature Fusion Module. In the feature fusion module, the text feature H_t and the image feature H_f are spliced together, and they are sent to the fully connected layer for fusion, and the fused features are sent to a gate control unit composed of two layers of fully connected neural networks. The control unit partially screens the fusion information, and finally outputs the fusion vector H_c.

Output Module. The output module uses the softmax classifier to predict the output probability of the label. The input fusion feature is H_c, and the output probability is $p(y)$.

$$p(y) = softmax(w_c H_c + b_c) \tag{6}$$

where w_c and b_c are the trained parameter matrices. The cross entropy loss function L_{CE} is as follows:

$$L_{CE} = \frac{1}{k} \sum_{i=1}^{k} t_i log(y_i) \tag{7}$$

where t $\in R^k$ is the one-hot represented truth tags and $y \in R^k$ is the estimated probability for each class by softmax, k is the number of target classes.

3.2 VST Model

The VST model receives text data and outputs text sequence labels. The label set is L = {B-ENT, I-ENT, O}, and the text sequence characters corresponding to the B-ENT and I-ENT are semantic tag. The model structure is shown in Fig. 3. First, the ROBERTA model is used to obtain the features of the text data, and then the text features are sent to a fully connected layer and CRF layer. Then calculate the emission probability and transition probability of the sequence label. Finally, the semantic tags are obtained according to the sequence label.

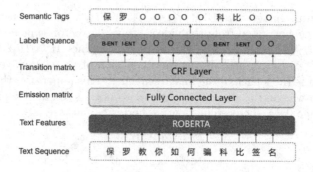

Fig. 3. VST model.

3.3 R-Drop Regularization

Dropout technique [7] is a commonly method in deep learning to prevent overfitting by simply dropping a certain proportion of hidden units from the neural network during training. R-Drop [13] is a effective regularization method built upon dropout, which adopts the bidirectional Kullback-Leibler (KL) divergence to adds a KL-divergence loss for the model. Given the training data x, R-Drop makes x go through the forward pass of the network twice and produces two distributions of the model predictions by the randomness of the dropout, denoted as P_1 (x) and P_2 (x). The calculation method of KL-divergence loss is as follows:

$$L_{KL} = \frac{1}{2} \left(D_{KL}(P_1(x)||P_2(x)) + D_{KL}(P_2(x)||P_1(x)) \right) \tag{8}$$

$$D_{KL}(A||B) = \sum A(x)log \left(\frac{A(x)}{B(x)} \right) \tag{9}$$

where L_{KL} is KL-divergence loss, and D_{KL} is the calculation formula of KL-divergence. Taking the VCT model as an example, the final loss function of the model is L_{All}:

$$L_{All} = L_{CE2} + \delta * L_{KL} \tag{10}$$

$$L_{CE2} = L_{CE}(P_1(x)) + L_{CE}(P_2(x)) \tag{11}$$

where δ is the coefficient weight to control L_{KL}, L_{CE} is the cross entropy loss, as shown in formula 7.

3.4 Model Integration

The integration process of models is shown in Fig. 4. First, the labeled data is randomly divided n times according to a ratio of 1:4 to obtain n groups data. Set different random seed values, and train to obtain M classification and extraction models. For classification tasks, the mode value of the predicted categories of all models is the final result. For the label extraction task, all the labels predicted by the models are counted, and labels with statistical values greater than K are selected as the final result. The choice of K value is related to the number of models M. In this ensemble method, the value of M is taken as 10 and the value of K is taken as 2.

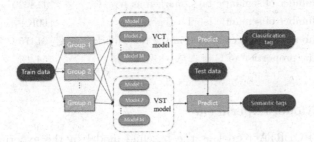

Fig. 4. Schematic diagram of model integration.

4   Experiment

4.1   Data Introduction

The data set contains 45,000 labeled data, 10,000 Test_A data, and 20,000 Test_B data. Each sample data includes video title, ASR (Automated Speech Recognition) text, OCR (Optical Character Recognition) text and the video feature matrix extracted by the pre-training model TSN [15]. The specific process of obtaining the video feature vector is in this project.[1] The data set supports two subtasks, and the first one is tag classification according to the video content, including the first-level tag classification and the second-level tag classification. The second is to extract the semantic tags of the video, and the types of tags include entities, concepts, events, and entities Attributes, etc. The statistical

---

[1] https://github.com/PaddlePaddle/Research/tree/master/KG/DuKEVU_Baseline.

results of the labeled data are shown in Table 1. There are a total of 33 first-level video tags, a total of 310 s-level video tags, a total of 118620 semantic tags, and 61475 tags completely contained in the text, accounting for 54.2% of the total number of tags.

In this paper, the labeled data is randomly divided into training data (80%) and test data (20%) for experimental analysis. We remove the duplicate content in the OCR text, intercept the last 150 characters in the OCR text, and intercept the first 150 characters in the ASR text data. The Title, ASR data and OCR data are spliced together to form the final text data.

The Chinese pre-training model ROBERTA used in all experiments comes from this project.[2]

Table 1. The statistical results of the labeled data.

Category	Amount
Number of first-level tags	33
Number of second-level tags	310
Number of semantic tags, marked as A	118620
Number of semantic label categories	60K+
Number of tags contained in the text, marked as C	61475
The proportion of C in A	54.2%

4.2   VCT Model Experiment

We use the ROERTA model as the baseline model in the experiments, and compare it with a variety of models and methods. The baseline model only uses the text data in the video with ROBERTA model and ignores other modal data. The Baseline-FF uses the first frame image vector of the video as the video feature, and fuses text features extracted by ROBERTA model for multi-modal classification. The Baseline-NeXtVLAD model uses the full amount of video data, adopts NeXtVLAD [15] to extract video features. The VCT model uses bidirectional LSTM and Attention to extract video features. The results of first-level tag classification and the second-level tag classification are shown in Table 2 and Table 3. We can get the following conclusions:

(1) Comparing the results of the Baseline and Baseline-FF models, it can be seen that the use of multi-modal data in the model can effectively improve the effect of tag classification.
(2) The VCT model has a better effect than the Baseline-NeXtVLAD model. The image module in the VCT model can better integrate video features, and the bidirectional LSTM model has much smaller parameters than the NeXtVLAD model. Baseline-NeXtVLAD uses the ROBERTA model

---

[2] https://github.com/ymcui/Chinese-BERT-wwm.

to extract text features, and the NeXtVLAD model integrates video features. The entire model has a large amount of parameters and is difficult to converge. This may be the cause of the poor performance of the Baseline-NeXtVLAD model.

(3) Using R-Drop regularization in model training can effectively improve the results of the model. The R-Drop method does not add any burden to the model in the inference phase, and only spends some time in the training phase.

Table 2. First-level tag classification.

Methods	F1
Baseline	0.7218
Baseline-FF	0.7346
Baseline-NeXtVLAD	0.7442
VCT (our model)	0.7494
Baseline + R-Drop	0.7328
Baseline-FF + R-Drop	0.7373
Baseline-NeXtVLAD + R-Drop	0.7511
VCT (our model) + R-Drop	0.7584

Table 3. Second-level tag classification.

Methods	F1
Baseline	0.5502
Baseline-FF	0.5552
Baseline-NeXtVLAD	0.5631
VCT (our model)	0.5814
Baseline + R-Drop	0.5593
Baseline-FF + R-Drop	0.567
Baseline-NeXtVLAD + R-Drop	0.5698
VCT (our model) + R-Drop	0.5886

4.3   VST Model Experiment

For video semantic tag task, we compares the ROBERTA model with our VST model in the experiments. From Table 4, it can be seen that the results of the VST model are better than the ROBERTA model, and the R-Drop regularization can effectively improve the results of the sequence labeling model.

Table 4. VST model experiment.

Methods	F1
ROBERTA	0.364
VST (our model)	0.381
VST (our model) + R-Drop	0.392

5   Conclusion

This paper builds a complete video semantic understanding system with VCT and VST model, and verifies the effectiveness of the VCT and VST model through experiments. In the CCKS2021 knowledge-enhanced video semantic understanding task, this system achieves an F1 score of 0.5054 with the Baseline-FF and VST model. The VCT model will further improve the system performance. In the part of video semantic tags, this system uses the VST model to extract tags from text data. According to Table 1, it can be seen that only 54.2% of the video semantic tags can be obtained directly through extraction. In the future, there will be a lot of room for improvement with multi-modal generation methods to obtain semantic tags.

References

1. Bertasius, G., Wang, H., Torresani, L.: Is space-time attention all you need for video understanding? arXiv preprint arXiv:2102.05095 (2021)
2. Devlin, J., Chang, M.W., Lee, K., Toutanova, K.: BERT: pre-training of deep bidirectional transformers for language understanding. arXiv preprint arXiv:1810.04805 (2018)
3. Feichtenhofer, C., Fan, H., Malik, J., He, K.: SlowFast networks for video recognition. In: Proceedings of the IEEE/CVF International Conference on Computer Vision, pp. 6202–6211 (2019)
4. Ging, S., Zolfaghari, M., Pirsiavash, H., Brox, T.: COOT: cooperative hierarchical transformer for video-text representation learning. arXiv preprint arXiv:2011.00597 (2020)
5. Graves, A., Mohamed, A.R., Hinton, G.: Speech recognition with deep recurrent neural networks. In: 2013 IEEE International Conference on Acoustics, Speech and Signal Processing, pp. 6645–6649. IEEE (2013)
6. He, D., et al.: StNet: local and global spatial-temporal modeling for action recognition. In: Proceedings of the AAAI Conference on Artificial Intelligence, vol. 33, pp. 8401–8408 (2019)
7. Hinton, G.E., Srivastava, N., Krizhevsky, A., Sutskever, I., Salakhutdinov, R.R.: Improving neural networks by preventing co-adaptation of feature detectors. arXiv preprint arXiv:1207.0580 (2012)
8. Huang, Z., Xu, W., Yu, K.: Bidirectional LSTM-CRF models for sequence tagging. arXiv preprint arXiv:1508.01991 (2015)
9. Kim, W., Son, B., Kim, I.: ViLT: vision-and-language transformer without convolution or region supervision. arXiv preprint arXiv:2102.03334 (2021)
10. Lafferty, J., McCallum, A., Pereira, F.C.: Conditional random fields: probabilistic models for segmenting and labeling sequence data (2001)
11. Li, L., Chen, Y.C., Cheng, Y., Gan, Z., Yu, L., Liu, J.: HERO: hierarchical encoder for video+ language omni-representation pre-training. arXiv preprint arXiv:2005.00200 (2020)
12. Li, X., Yan, H., Qiu, X., Huang, X.: FLAT: Chinese NER using flat-lattice transformer. arXiv preprint arXiv:2004.11795 (2020)
13. Liang, X., et al.: R-Drop: regularized dropout for neural networks. arXiv preprint arXiv:2106.14448 (2021)
14. Lin, J., Gan, C., Han, S.: TSM: temporal shift module for efficient video understanding. In: Proceedings of the IEEE/CVF International Conference on Computer Vision, pp. 7083–7093 (2019)
15. Lin, R., Xiao, J., Fan, J.: NextVLAD: an efficient neural network to aggregate frame-level features for large-scale video classification. In: Proceedings of the European Conference on Computer Vision (ECCV) Workshops (2018)

16. Lison, P., Hubin, A., Barnes, J., Touileb, S.: Named entity recognition without labelled data: a weak supervision approach. arXiv preprint arXiv:2004.14723 (2020)
17. Liu, Y., et al.: RoBERTa: a robustly optimized BERT pretraining approach. arXiv preprint arXiv:1907.11692 (2019)
18. Luo, H., et al.: UniVL: a unified video and language pre-training model for multi-modal understanding and generation. arXiv preprint arXiv:2002.06353 (2020)
19. Luo, H., et al.: CLIP4Clip: an empirical study of clip for end to end video clip retrieval. arXiv preprint arXiv:2104.08860 (2021)
20. Vaswani, A., et al.: Attention is all you need. In: Advances in Neural Information Processing Systems, pp. 5998–6008 (2017)
21. Yang, Z., et al.: XLNet: generalized autoregressive pretraining for language understanding. In: Advances in Neural Information Processing Systems, vol. 32 (2019)
22. Zhou, P., et al.: Attention-based bidirectional long short-term memory networks for relation classification. In: Proceedings of the 54th Annual Meeting of the Association for Computational Linguistics (volume 2: Short Papers), pp. 207–212 (2016)
23. Zhu, L., Yang, Y.: ActBERT: learning global-local video-text representations. In: Proceedings of the IEEE/CVF Conference on Computer Vision and Pattern Recognition, pp. 8746–8755 (2020)

An Integrated Method of Semantic Parsing and Information Retrieval for Knowledge Base Question Answering

Shiqi Zhen[✉], Xianwei Yi, Zhishu Lin, Weiqi Xiao, Haibo Su, and Yijing Liu

Cognitive Intelligence LabPercent Technology, Wuhan 430073, China
{shiqi.zhen,xianwei.yi,zhishu.lin,weiqi.xiao,haibo.su,
yijing.liu}@percent.cn

Abstract. For the task of open domain Knowledge Base Question Answering (KBQA) in CCKS 2021, we propose an integrated method, which complementarily combines a more generalized information retrieval model and a more accurate semantic parsing model without manual involvement of templates. Our method achieves the averaged F1-score of 78.52% on the final test data, and ranks third in the KBQA task of CCKS 2021.

Keywords: KBQA · Information retrieval · Semantic parsing

1 Introduction

Knowledge Base Question Answering (KBQA), which aims to answer natural language questions over a knowledge base such as Freebase, has become a popular application of NLP technologies. For example, given a question "莫妮卡·贝鲁奇的代表作？", its answer can be found from the fact triple [<莫妮卡·贝鲁奇><代表作品><西西里的美丽传说>].

There are two mainstream methods: information retrieval and semantic parsing. In the traditional information retrieval (IR) methods, the entity mention in question is first identified by sequence labeling and then linked to the entity in the knowledge base (called topic entity). Starting from the topic entity, a question-specific path from KB is extracted as a candidate path. Afterwards, candidate paths are ranked by their semantic similarity to the question and the best candidate path is selected to answer the question [1, 2]. The semantic parsing (SP) method directly resolves the question into an executable query statement for knowledge base, such as SPARQL. Traditional semantic parsing usually relies on expensive predefined templates by experts or syntactic parsing like dependencies. Errors in syntactic parsing will be propagated to the downstream semantic parsing and affect overall performance [3, 4].

In this paper, we propose a combined method, which applies semantic parsing to deal with questions with fixed sentence patterns or functions such as "filter", and applies information retrieval to deal with questions with diverse sentence patterns. In information retrieval module, the pipeline consists of four sub-modules, namely mention recognition, entity linking, path generation and path ranking. In semantic parsing module, we adopt

B. Qin et al. (Eds.): CCKS 2021, CCIS 1553, pp. 44–51, 2022.
https://doi.org/10.1007/978-981-19-0713-5_6

two methods: SPARQL template matching and SPARQL generation. SPARQL template matching is to match the most similar SPARQL template which is automatically generated from the training set, and SPARQL generation utilizes pre-trained language model (PLM) to generate new SPARQL. Finally, we integrate semantic parsing module and information retrieval module by selecting answers in the same way. The workflow of the proposed method in this paper is illustrated in Fig. 1.

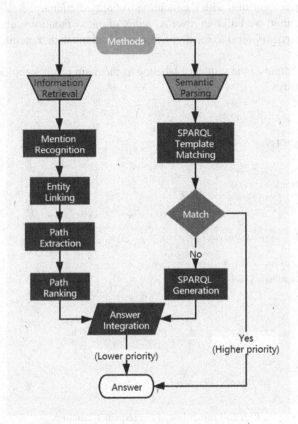

Fig. 1. Workflow of our proposed method.

2 Method

2.1 Information Retrieval

2.1.1 Mention Recognition

The goal of mention recognition is to recognize the text fragments of the KB entity mentioned in the question. In order to improve the recall rate, we have implemented four ways of mention recognition.

(1) Sequence Labeling: as shown in Fig. 2, we model mention recognition as a sequence labeling task and train a K-Fold cross-validated sequence labeling model based on Roberta + CRF;

(2) Rule-based Recognition: we use regular expressions to match special entities and attribute values such as dates, continuous English, and text fragments in quotation marks, etc.;

(3) Dictionary-based Recognition: we identify the mentions in the question by the longest match algorithm with the mention-to-entity dictionary;

(4) Fuzzy matching: we build an inverted index of entity mentions, and then use the question as a query term to recall the top ten mentions with matching degree.

We take the output of the sequence labeling as the main result, supplemented by the results of other ways.

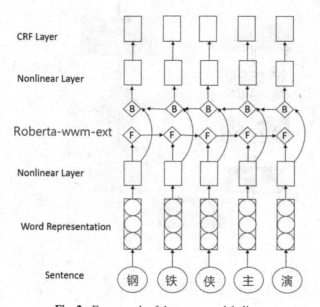

Fig. 2. Framework of the sequence labeling.

2.1.2 Entity Linking

Given the result of mention recognition, based on the mention-to-entity dictionary and inverted index, the entity reference is mapped to the node in the knowledge graph, and the candidates of the entity linking are generated. In order to improve the accuracy of entity linking, we extract the neighbor nodes and relations of the candidate entity as additional information. To restrict the number of neighbor nodes and relations, we adopt PageRank algorithm [5] to evaluate the importance of nodes. We follow two assumptions: (1) the greater the in-degree of an entity node, the higher the importance of the entity; (2) the higher the importance of the source node linked to an entity node, the higher the entity importance. We keep the neighbor nodes (and relations) with top 10 PageRank scores as additional neighbor information.

We use a pre-trained language model for semantic matching calculation. The input form of the entity linking model is "[CLS][Question][SEP]Mention&Entity#Neighbor information[SEP]". In order to recall the correct path as much as possible, we keep top 10 candidate entities.

2.1.3 Path Extraction

Path Extraction aims to extract candidate paths from the knowledge base based on candidate entities.

Given a single entity, we adopt the following path patterns:

(1) <entity><relation><?x>;
(2) <?x><relation><entity>;
(3) <entity><relation_1><?x><?x><relation_2><?y>;
(4) <entity><relation_1><?x><?y><relation_2><?x>;
(5) <?x><relation_1><entity><?x><relation_2><?y>;
(6) <?x><relation_1><entity><?y><relation_2><?x>.

Given multiple entities, we adopt the following path patterns (taking two entities as an example):

(1) <entity_1><relation_1><?x><entity_2><relation_2><?x>;
(2) <?x><relation_1><entity_1><?x><relation_2><entity_2>;
(3) <?x><relation_1><entity_1><entity_2><relation_2><?x>;
(4) <entity_1><relation_1><?x><?x><relation_2><entity_2>;
(5) (1)/(2)/(3)/(4)+<?x><relation_3><?y>;
(6) (1)/(2)/(3)/(4)+<?y><relation_3><?x>;
(7) <entity_1><?x><entity_2>.

In order to avoid too many candidate paths for recall, we propose the following pruning strategies:

(1) delete the path where the answer entity is the topic entity;
(2) if the number of two-hop nodes of a node exceeds 10000, no two-hop traversal will be performed on this node;
(3) when the number of two-hop paths (out or in) exceeds 100 but less than 500, delete the candidate path that has no character intersection between the relation and the question in the two-hop paths;
(4) when the number of two-hop paths (out or in) exceeds 500, delete all two-hop paths.

2.1.4 Path Ranking

The path ranking module calculates the semantic similarity degree between the question and the candidate path. The candidate path with higher similarity is more likely to get the correct answer to the question. Considering the large number of candidate paths extracted, we use the LightGBM model that incorporates the following features to sort the candidate paths and keep top 20 paths:

Literal features: the number of coincidences of path and question in characters (or words); Jaccard similarity between path and question in characters (or words); Levenshtein Distance between path and question in characters (or words); whether all the characters of path are in the question;

Popularity features: popularity of the answer entity; the number of different one-hop relations of the answer entity;

Number features: the number of overlapping numbers in path and question; Jaccard similarity between path and question in numbers; whether all the numbers of path are in the question;

Path features: the number of answer entities; the number of entities; the number of relations; the length of path;

Semantic features: vector similarity at character level between path and question; vector similarity at bi-gram level between path and question; vector similarity at word level between path and question;

Other features: whether the words within the special symbols ("" and 《》, etc.) in the question appear in the path; whether the answer entity is in question; the position of the answer entity in the path; whether the relations of path are in question; whether the target relation of path is in question.

To get a better similarity result, we remove subordinate elements in the candidate path. we only keep the topic entity and relation of the path, and we replace the answer node as symbol "^". For example, given a question "亚马孙河所在的大洲主要使用哪些语言",

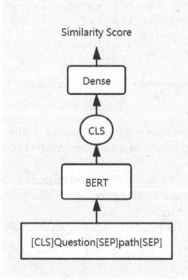

Fig. 3. Framework of re-rank model.

we replace its candidate path "<亚马孙河><所属地区><?x><?x><语言><?y>" with "亚马孙河所属地区语言^". Then, we use BERT to re-rank the similarity score between the candidate path and the question. The framework is shown in Fig. 3.

2.2 Semantic Parsing

2.2.1 SPARQL Template Matching

SPARQL template matching aims to generate accurate SPARQL via the SPARQL template achieved from the training dataset. It mainly includes the following steps: 1) abstract query generation; 2) SPARQL template generation; 3) query and SPARQL template match; 4) SPARQL generation. The first step is to transform the query (question) into an abstract query. The abstract query is a query whose mention is replaced by Part-of-Speech (POS). In the meanwhile, the SPARQL corresponding to the abstract query also replace the entity with POS. After that, we can achieve SPARQL templates with entity slots. For one test instance, we first transform the query into an abstract query and then calculating the similarity score between the test abstract query and all abstract queries achieved from the training dataset. The SPARQL template with the highest similarity score will be chosen as goal SPARQL template. To get the final SPARQL, the slot in the goal SPARQL template is replaced with the corresponding mention in the test query.

2.2.2 SPARQL Generation

In the case of unsuccessful SPARQL template matching, we utilize Unified Language Model (UniLM) [6] to directly generate SPARQL. We pre-train the UniLM with whole entity (or relation) masking in SPARQL and fine-tune UniLM. Considering that the entity or relation in SPARQL generated directly by fine-tuned UniLM may not exist in KG, we adopt 4 revision strategies to recover the correct entities and relations:

(1) when the entity does not exist, use the entities obtained by fuzzy matching to replace the original entity; when the relation does not exist, use adjacent relations of the entity that is similar to the original relation to replace the original relation;
(2) when the relation does not exist, use the relations obtained by fuzzy matching and synonym dictionary to replace the original relation; when the entity does not exist, use adjacent entities of the relation that is similar to the original entity to replace the original entity;
(3) regardless of whether the original entity (or relation) exists, the entity (or relation) after fuzzy matching is used to replace the original entity (or relation);
(4) add the Regex function in SPARQL to automatically complete the non-existent entity.

2.3 Answer Integration

In this section, we integrate the results of information retrieval and semantic parsing. We utilize the re-rank model in Sect. 2.1.4 to score the executable SPARQL that can return answers. Therefore, the results of information retrieval and semantic parsing are scored by the same model. We choose the result with the highest score of the two methods as the final answer.

3   Experiments and Results

3.1   Dataset and Experimental Settings

Our method is evaluated on the CCKS 2021 dataset. The dataset involves encyclopedia, medical and life service fields. Especially, the dataset in the field of life service involves functions such as filtering and sorting. The training set has 6525 questions with labeled SPARQLs and answers, the dev set has 2100 questions, and the test set has 1191 questions. The given knowledge graph contains 66 million triples and more than 20 million entities.

We use ElasticSearch to build an inverted index. The whole knowledge graph is stored in Nebula graph database. Our BERT model uses RoBERTa-wwm-ext-large uniformly.

3.2   Mention Recognition Evaluation

As shown in Table 1, we evaluate the unsupervised mention recognition method on the whole training dataset.

Table 1. Result of unsupervised mention recognition

	Rule-based	Dictionary-based	Fuzzy matching	All
Precision	0.7949	0.3136	0.5719	0.2773
Recall	0.0571	0.7016	0.5040	0.8537

3.3   Path Extraction Evaluation

For the training dataset, we extract about 7,000,000 candidate paths. Among them, there are about 11,000 correct paths, covering 75% of the questions in the training dataset. For the test dataset, we extract about 2,500,000 candidate paths.

3.4   SPARQL Generation Evaluation

Table 2 shows the SPARQL generation performance of experimentation on 20% of training dataset. From the comparison, we can find that the pre-training and revise strategies have a great effect. Especially the first revise strategy (revise-1) shows the biggest improvement, which illustrates that the entity confidence and reference in the directly generated SPARQL is very large.

Table 2. Result of SPARQL generation

Method	F1-score
Our model	81.3%
Our model w/o pre-training	79.5%
Our model w/o revise-1	72.3%
Our model w/o revise-2	79.8%
Our model w/o revise-3	80.5%
Our model w/o revise-4	80.3%

4 Conclusion

We introduce an KBQA system in this paper. The system combines two mainstream methods: information retrieval and semantic parsing. The information retrieval consists of four steps: mention recognition, entity linking, path extraction and path ranking. The semantic parsing contains SPARQL template matching and SPARQL generation. Finally, our system obtains an average F1-score of 78.52 on the test data, and ranks third in the KBQA task of CCKS 2021. Specifically, the score of the first ranked team is 78.86 and the score of the second ranked team is 78.79. In the future, we intend to optimize our path ranking method so that it can select the correct answer more accurately.

References

1. Yao, X., Van Durme, B.: Information extraction over structured data: Question answering with freebase. In: Proceedings of the 52nd Annual Meeting of the Association for Computational Linguistics (Volume 1: Long Papers). (2014)
2. Bordes, A., Chopra, S., Weston, J.: Question answering with subgraph embeddings. arXiv preprint arXiv:1406.3676 (2014)
3. Abujabal, A., Yahya, M., Riedewald, M., Weikum, G.: Automated template generation for question answering over knowledge graphs. In WWW **2017**, 1191–1200 (2017)
4. Berant, J., et al.: Semantic parsing on freebase from question-answer pairs. In: Proceedings of the 2013 Conference on Empirical Methods in Natural Language Processing (2013)
5. Page, L.B., et al.: The PageRank citation ranking: bringing order to the web. In: Stanford Digital Libraries Working Paper (1998)
6. Dong, L., Yang, N., Wang, W., et al.: Unified Language Model Pre-training for Natural Language Understanding and Generation (2019)

Basic Profiling Extraction Based on XGBoost

Wenhan Yang[1]([⊠]), Boyu Sun[1], and Banruo Liu[2]

[1] Beijing University of Posts and Telecommunications, Beijing, China
2019213705@bupt.edu.cn
[2] Tsinghua University, Beijing, China

Abstract. With the deepening of human academic research in various fields and the diversification of research branches, it has become an important work to obtain the information of scholars in the same field and conduct reference research on their research results. Thus, it is of vital importance to obtain relevant scholar information through information extraction and prediction by the result of search engines. Through XGBoost, KNN, information extraction and other methods, we realized the function of predicting scholars' home page, email address, language, gender, title and other information through the search engine search results of scholars' names and institutions, and achieved high accuracy in some aspects.

Keywords: XGBoost · Scholar profiling

1 XGBoost

1.1 Introduction

The XGBoost [1] model was first proposed in XGBoost: A Scalable Tree Boosting System in 2016, and is still one of the most useful models for solving classification problems so far. The winning teams in data mining and machine learning competitions have mostly used XGBoost systems to solve practical problems such as web content categorizing, advertising bidding ranking, and customer behavior prediction, demonstrating a wide range of applications. Based on the above analysis, this article uses XGBoost as the basic tool.

The main characteristics of the proposed algorithm are as follows.

- XGBoost has good anti-overfitting characteristics.
- XGBoost has high computational efficiency.
- The calculation process of XGBoost has certain enlightenment.

1.2 Basic Theory

The algorithm idea of XGBOOST model is to continuously iterate with trees. Each time a new tree is added, it is to fit the residual error predicted last time. In this way, we can obtain K decision trees, drop the samples we want to predict onto the corresponding leaf nodes of each tree, and add their scores to obtain the predicted value we want to get.

B. Qin et al. (Eds.): CCKS 2021, CCIS 1553, pp. 52–58, 2022.
https://doi.org/10.1007/978-981-19-0713-5_7

2 Homepage

2.1 Introduction

The dataset provides two types of scholar homepage, one is the official homepage maintained by the scholar's institution and the other is maintained by the scholar personally. In order to filter the scholar's home page from the web page presented by Google search engine, we design a binary classifier trained with XGBoost machine learning model. We input combination of features of homepage and semantic representation of abstract of web page to train the classifier.

2.2 Feature Design

Based on the actual situation,we took into account following information to design features: scholar information including name and organization and web page information including URLs, titles of the HTML files and HTML text contents.

After data cleaning for all of the text as input, including removal of punctuations and garbled characters, lower case processing, stop word processing and Chinese to Pinyin, we design these features:

1. The ranking of URL in Google search. The higher the ranking, the more relevant the pages are to scholars.
2. Number of positive key words in the URL. For example, URL ending in 'faculty', 'homepage' have a positive effect on home page decisions. The positive key words are listed in the appendix.
3. Number of positive key words in title of a HTML file.
4. Number of negative key words in the URL. For instance, URL containing 'LinkedIn', 'Google scholar' etc. may less likely to be the homepage of a scholar. The negative key words are listed in the appendix.
5. Number of negative key words in the title of a HTML file.
6. Whether or not the URL contains 'edu'. If yes, this feature is assigned a value of 1.
7. Whether or not the URL contains 'org'. If yes, this feature is assigned a value of 1.
8. Whether or not the URL contains 'gov'. If yes, this feature is assigned a value of 1.
9. Whether or not the URL contains 'google. If yes, this feature is assigned a value of 1.
10. Percentage of name in the URL. For example, given a name 'Bell John' and a URL 'www.google.scholar/bell', the feature is assigned a value of 50%.
11. Percentage of organization names in the URL. For example, given an organization name 'Department of Chemistry, Tsinghua University' and a URL 'http://www.chem.tsinghua.edu.cn/info/1101/2737.htm', the feature is assigned a value of 25% with 'Tsinghua' of 'Department Chemistry Tsinghua University'.
12. All text Length of each HTML file.
13. Text length of title in a HTML file.
14. Percentage of name in the title of the HTML file.
15. The ratio of the length of the name to the length of the HTML file text.
16. Total of number of every word of name appearing in the HTML file text.
17. Percentage of organization names in the title of the HTML file.
18. The ratio of the length of the organization to the length of the HTML file text.

2.3 Semantic Representation:

TFIDF is a common weighting technique used in information retrieval and information exploration. It is a statistical method used to assess the importance of a word to one of the documents in a document set or a corpus. The importance of a word is proportional to the number of times it appears in the document and inversely proportional to the number of times it appears in the entire corpus. Under each item in Google's search results is an abstract of the page. In our work, we call TfidfVectorizer from the Sklearn package to represent the text characteristics of the abstract of each web page.

Abstract of all retrieval results of Google search are extracted as corpus after data cleaning, and each abstract is converted into semantic vector by TFIDF algorithm. The semantic vectors are concatenated with feature vectors. Input the vectors, we trained XGBoost model and then evaluate model effects on validation sets.

We trained the XGBoost model using these features and achieved 43% accuracy on the validation set.

3 Email

3.1 Introduction

The prefix of the general mailbox is related to the name, which may be the abbreviation of the last name or given name. The suffix is related to the organization. We extract all the emails by regex matching from HTML files and normalize the email format to preserve the correspondence between the email and the source web page. Then we design the features of email based on scholars' names, organizations and web pages, using XGBoost to classify features. Therefore, the scholar's emails are selected.

3.2 Email Feature Selection

Like homepage, we also design some features to classify the scholar's e-mail. The features are as following:

1. The length of organization
2. The length of email
3. The ratio of the longest common string of the name and prefix to the name. For example, given an email 'zhangbm@mail.tsinghua.edu.cn' and a name 'Boming Zhang', the feature is assigned a value of 5/11 because the common string of name and prefix of email is "zhang". The length of "zhang" divided by length of 'Boming Zhang' is 5/11.
4. The ratio of the longest common string of the name and prefix to the name Percentage of name in the title of the HTML file.
5. The ratio of the longest common string of the first name and prefix to the first name.
6. The ratio of the longest common string of the last and prefix to the first name.
7. The ratio of the longest common string of the name abbreviation and prefix to the name abbreviation. Abbreviation is formed by combining the first letters of each of the first and last name in sequence.

8. The ratio of the longest common string of the first name abbreviation and prefix to the first name abbreviation.
9. The ratio of the number of occurrences in the suffix of each word in the organization to the length of organization.

Besides, we need to take the features of web page from which the emails come into account. Therefore, the features 1, 12–18 of homepage part are concatenated together.

We trained the XGBoost model using these features and achieved 55% accuracy on the validation set.

4 Language

4.1 Introduction

Google search renders web pages mostly in English. Due to the limitation of dataset, we decided to train a RNN model to classify the language according to scholar's name.

4.2 Language Selection

At first we just used API that AMINER provides to us, which can tell how many languages one could speak and the probability only given one's name. Usually, many scholars' language is English according to our dataset. Thus, with scholar's name and organization as input we selected the language except for English whose probability higher than a man-made threshold. Otherwise, we selected English as the output. This approach results in an accuracy about 60% in validation set.

4.3 Adaption of Name-Ethnicity Classification

Another perception told us that one' native language is highly related with one's name. And one application of NLP, the Name-Ethnicity Classification [2] seems to fit well in our topic. Thus, we adapt the approach of using character n-gram RNN(Jinhyuk Lee, et al. 2017) to fit in our work, the Name-Language Classification.

In detail, we use a bidirectional LSTM as basic model. We transform one's name into lower case alphabets and insert token of position meaning between the words. Then we extract the 1,2,3-g of the transformed token sequence respectively and feed them into 3 independent embedding layer and LSTM respectively. Then we concatenate the final state of hidden layer, and use a softmax to generate the final output.

This method achieved about 70% accuracy in the validation set.

5 Gender

5.1 Introduction

The prediction of gender can be seen as a kind of binary classification. We used several methods to predict the gender of the scholars including Decision Tree Classifier, SVM, Logistic Regression, Random Forest Classifier and KNN.

5.2 Gender Feature Selection

To get the features, we firstly got the titles and abstractions in the google search pages and made a corpus of abstractions of every scholar. After that, we extracted following features:

1. The term frequency and inverse document frequency of word his and word her in the corpus.
2. A number representing whether the word his and her is in the first k words in the corpus respectively. If the return value is 1, it represent that the word is in the first k words, if the return value is 0, it represent that the word is not in the first k words.
3. The co-occurrence frequency between the word his and organization name of the scholar in the corpus, the co-occurrence frequency between the word her and the organization name of the scholar in the corpus.
4. The co-occurrence frequency between the word his and the first name of the scholar in the titles and corpus respectively, The co-occurrence frequency between the word her and the first name of the scholar in the titles and corpus respectively.
5. The co-occurrence frequency between the word his and the last name of the scholar in the titles and corpus respectively, The co-occurrence frequency between the word her and the last name of the scholar in the titles and corpus respectively.

5.3 Selection of Classification Models

For the selection of classification models, we used five classification models in total: Decision Tree Classifier, SVM, Logistic Regression, Random Forest Classifier and KNN. The accuracy of Decision Tree Classifier is 89%, The accuracy of SVM is 90%, the accuracy of Logistic Regression is 86%, the accuracy of Random Forest Classifier is 90% and the accuracy of KNN is 91%. Thus, finally, we chose KNN as our final selection.

6 Title

6.1 Introduction

To predict the title of the scholars, we extracted the abstractions and contents of every google search page, and then, extracted information about titles and predict the title of the scholars according to the known information.

6.2 Title Prediction

Firstly, we extracted the title, abstraction and content of every google search page, then, we check if the text is valid for the extraction of title by checking the existence score of the name in the text, if the whole name is in the text, the score will be 1, if the last name or the first name is in the text, the score will be 0.5, if none of the first name or last name is in the text, the score will be 0. If the existence score of name is greater than 0.2, we will use that text and check if the text have the titles we expected like professor, associate professor, assistant professor, etc. Finally, we will check the frequency of appearance of every title, and the title that appear most will be chose as the title we predicted.

7 Evaluation

After constructing our model, we divided the extracted data into training sets and testing sets in a ratio of 4:1. The evaluation indicators for each aspect on the test set are as following table.

As for final evaluation givn by the authority, the criterion is more strict. Each scholar has a total of K (k = 5 in this task) personal portrait data to be evaluated. All of them are evaluated by the way of perfect match. The score of perfect match is 1, otherwise it is 0. Since homepage and Email are a collection, the similarity between the extracted collection and the collection given by the marked answer is calculated by Jaccard index (i.e. the number of elements in the intersection of two collections divided by the number of elements in the union of two collections). The final score of the predicted value of a scholar's portrait data is the average of the k predicted scores. A contestant's final score on this task is the average of the predicted scores for each scholar's portrait data. That is (Table 1):

$$\text{score} = \frac{1}{kN} \sum_{i=1}^{N} \sum_{j=1}^{k} s_i$$

Table 1. Evaluation on the test set of extracted data

Information	Accuracy	Recall	Precision
Homepage	91.0%	89.3%	79.4%
Email	88.7%	92%	84.2%
Language	91.1%	90.0	87.4%
Gender	94.0%	90.1%	89.6%
Title	93.8	87.3%	90.9%
Final Evaluation	0.66777		rank(7/18)

However, the final evaluation is much worse than ours because of imbalance of data label used for binary classification.

8 Conclusion

To sum up, using different methods, we achieved the task of predicting scholars' information. We used XGBoost model to predict scholar's homepage and email, finally achieved an accuracy of 43% and 55% in homepage prediction and email prediction respectively. For the prediction of language, RNN model is used to classify the scholar's language according to their name and we achieved an accuracy of 70%. For the prediction of gender, several methods are used including Decision Tree Classifier, SVM, Logistic Regression, Random Forest Classifier and KNN, finally, we achieved the highest accuracy of 91% using KNN model. For the prediction of title, using basic frequency extraction, we achieved an accuracy of 50%. Basically, we achieved these tasks using different methods, however, there still exists some problems in our methods, for instance, there are some problems caused by anti-crawling mechanism such as missing information in official HTML files, so our existing work did not make full use of the actual results of search engines. In the follow-up work, we will try to obtain complete web page information by using better crawler techniques such as HTML simulation login to complete the data set, so as to improve the training effect of classifier. It is expected that our accuracy can be further improved through subsequent processing.

Appendix

The positive key words include 'edu', 'faculty', 'id', 'staff', 'detail', 'person', 'about', 'academic', 'teacher', 'list', 'people', 'lish', 'homepages', 'researcher', 'team', 'teachers', 'member', 'profile'.

The negative key words include 'books', 'google', 'pdf', 'esc', 'scholar', 'netprofile', 'linkedin', 'researchgate', 'news', 'article', 'wikipedia', 'gov', 'showrating', 'youtube', 'blots', 'citation', 'expert', 'dblp', 'researchgate', 'baidu', 'aminer', 'irps', 'taobao'.

References

1. Chen, T., Guestrin, C.: XGBoost: a scalable tree boosting system. In: ACM SIGKDD International Conference on Knowledge Discovery and Data Mining. ACM, pp. 785–794 (2016)
2. Lee, J., Kim, H., Ko, M., Choi, D., Choi, J., Kang, J.: Name nationality classification with recurrent neural networks. In: IJCAI, pp. 2081–2087 (2017)

Data Augmentation Based on Pre-trained Language Model for Event Detection

Meng Zhang, Zhiwen Xie, and Jin Liu$^{(\boxtimes)}$

School of Computer Science, Wuhan University, Wuhan 430072, China
{zhangm,xiezhiwen,jinliu}@whu.edu.cn

Abstract. Event detection (ED) is an important task which needs to identify the event triggers in the sentence and classify the event types. For the general fine-grained event detection task, we propose an event detection scheme based on pre-trained model, combined with data augmentation and pseudo labelling method, which improves the event detection ability of the model. At the same time, we use voting for model ensemble, so as to effectively utilize the advantages of multiple models. Our model achieves F1 score of 69.86% on the test set of CCKS2021 general fine-grained event detection task and ranks the third place in the competition.

Keywords: Event detection · Pre-trained model · Data augmentation · Pseudo labelling

1 Introduction

Event detection is an important task in information extraction. It aims at recognizing event triggers from sentences and classifying event types [17]. The **event** is the condition that prompts changes in the state of things and relationships [8], and it has a label called **event type**. The **event trigger** is the main word or phrase that most clearly expresses the occurrence of an event [3]. Furthermore, there are also two stages in event detection, which are called **trigger identification** and **trigger classification** [6]. For instance, in the sentence "He **approached** with excess speed and **braked** too late", "approached" and "braked" should be recognized as event triggers in trigger identification phase and respectively belong to the event type of "Arriving" and "Self_motion" in trigger classification phase.

At present, online social media has become an important channel to obtain information because of its high real-time ability, so there is a need to monitor the security and correctness of the information. Event detection can be used for network public opinion monitoring and early warning. It mainly identifies phrases with high public opinion value and then we can take measures in a short time which maintains the safety of public.

© Springer Nature Singapore Pte Ltd. 2022
B. Qin et al. (Eds.): CCKS 2021, CCIS 1553, pp. 59–68, 2022.
https://doi.org/10.1007/978-981-19-0713-5_8

Some models have shown encouraging results in event detection, but there are still some limitations that hinder the development of event detection. Although compared to ACE 2005 dataset [16], the dataset in our task is larger and has more diverse event types, it is still difficult to train a robust model. Data augmentation refers to the method of increasing data for training model without collecting or manually generating [9]. In some cases especially few-shot learning, data augmentation shows significant improvement due to the increasement of training samples. When training models with supervised learning, the data needs to be labelled and actually it is expensive and difficult to obtain. Pseudo labelling is one of the semi-supervised learning techniques. In pseudo labelling, unlabelled data can be labelled by models trained with labelled data, and combined with labelled data, the model will be more robust. Inspired by these strategies, we conduct research on this aspect in the competition, such as data augmentation and pseudo labelling. Besides that, due to the advantages of the pre-trained model in feature representation, our model is mainly based on it. In summary, our contributions of this paper are as follows:

- We model event detection task as a sequence tagging problem, and use the pre-trained model for training.
- In terms of data, in order to enable the model to learn more abundant features, we use data augmentation based on the pre-trained BERT model and pseudo labelling.
- In prediction phase, we use voting method to combine the prediction results of multiple models.
- We apply the above methods to the CCKS2021 general fine-grained event detection task, and finally achieve F1 score of 69.86% on test set and rank the third place in the competition.

Next, we will introduce related work, methods, experiments and conclusions respectively.

2   Related Work

Event detection plays a crucial role in the scope of NLP and many efforts have been devoted to ED in recent years. Feature-based models aim at how to extract valuable features. Ahn et al. extract lexical features, dependency features, Word-Net features, context features and related entity features of candidates in trigger identification, which achieve promising results [1]. Ji et al. propose a cross-document event extraction framework not only focuses on the influence of current document, but also the related documents to revise the original result and improve the event extraction task [11]. Based on the framework, Liao et al. use information of other event types to help to make predictions [13]. Although feature-based models show desireable performance, they need to manually design how to extract features and rely on existing knowledge such as WordNet [15].

With the development of deep learning, many researches are based on neural network to solve the ED task, which show significant progress than models that obtain features manually. Chen et al. propose the CNN-based model DMCNN [2]. In this model, the dynamic multi-pooling layer can retain more valuable information than traditional CNN model. Compared to CNN-based models, some RNN-based models such as LSTM [10] and BiLSTM(Bidirectional LSTM) can retain useful features selectively. Furthermore, BiLSTM can efficiently use both past and future input features. When using these models, we obtain hidden states to classify event types. With the development of pre-training technique, pre-trained models such as BERT [5] obtain general feature representation from a large amount of unlabelled data and have achieved excellent results in many natural language processing tasks, so that we can directly fine-tune based on the pre-trained model with our data. Moreover, because of using the Masked Language Model(MLM), pre-trained models like BERT [5] and RoBERTa [14] can predict the masked words according to the context, which provide ideas for data augmentation.

3   Method

3.1   Task Definition

For a given set of English plain text documents $D = \{d_1, d_2, ..., d_c\}$, and candidate triggers(contains event triggers and non-event triggers) $t = \{t_1, t_2, ...t_m\}$, we need to identify all event triggers and classify the corresponding event types. Tabel 1 shows the sample data.

Table 1. Sample data

Document	The 2006 Pangandaran earthquake and tsunami occurred on July 17 at along a subduction zone off the coast of west and central Java, a large and densely populated island in the Indonesian archipelago
Candidate triggers	earthquake, tsunami, occurred, populated, Pangandaran, July, subduction, zone, coast, west, central, Java, large, densely, island, Indonesian, archipelago
Event triggers	earthquake, Event type: Catastrophe tsunami, Event type: Catastrophe occurred, Event type: Presence
Non-event triggers	populated, Pangandaran, July, subduction, zone, coast, west, central, Java, large, densely, island, Indonesian, archipelago

As shown in Table 1, **earthquake, tsunami** and **occurred** are event triggers in the document, and the event types belong to **catastrophe, catastrophe** and **presence** respectively, while other candidate triggers are non-event triggers, and the type is none.

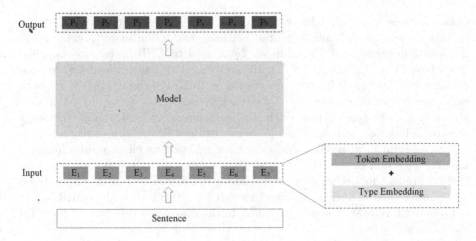

Fig. 1. Event detection model

3.2 Event Detection Model

In this competition we use pre-trained language models, including BERT [5], ELECTRA [4], RoBERTa [14], SpanBERT [12], UniLM [7] and XLNet [18]. The input of our model is the sentence and the tags of tokens distinguishing whether the token belongs to candidate triggers. Then we add them after embedding separately and input into the model. For the output of our model, we use a linear layer to convert dimension and get the score of all pre-defined types. Finally, we calculate the type with the highest score in each token to generate the final predictions. Figure 1 shows the overall framework.

For the loss function in this task, we adopt the CrossEntropyLoss that measures the distance between real distribution and prediction distribution. Let the prediction distribution of a token be $p = \{p_0, p_1, ..., p_{k-1}\}$ and the real distribution be $q = \{q_0, q_1, ..., q_{k-1}\}$ where k represents the number of labels, the CrossEntropyLoss of one token is shown in Eq(1), and the total loss is sum of each token loss in the sentence.

$$Loss = \sum_{i=0}^{n-1} q_i log(p_i) \tag{1}$$

3.3 Data Augmentation

To ensure the model learn richer features, we use data augmentation in the competition. Data augmentation methods that we commonly use include word replacement, reverse translation, etc. According to the dataset, we choose a method of randomly replacing words to train more robust models and improve performance. Firstly, we randomly choose words from the sentence and replace each of these words with the "[MASK]" tag. Then we use the pre-trained BERT

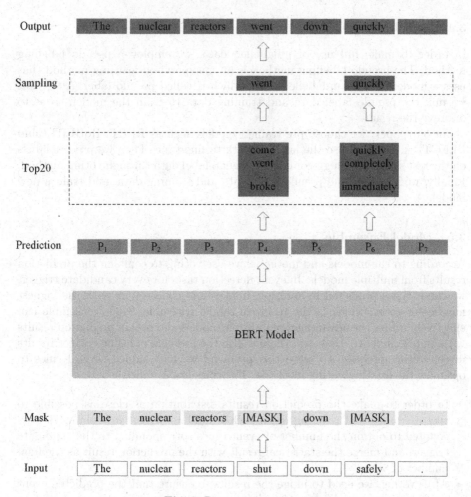

Fig. 2. Data augmentation

model to predict the "[MASK]" part. Finally, we randomly select a word from the top 20 words with highest prediction scores to replace the "[MASK]" tag. We repeat this operation many times to generate multiple copies of data. Figure 2 shows the data augmentation method.

In the training phase, we randomly choose a piece of data in the first n epoches and add it into the original training set, which enables the model to learn richer features and enhance the generalization ability of it. After n epoches, in order to avoid the influence of noise in generated data, the data we generated is no longer used for training. With the data augmentation method based on the pre-trained BERT model, we get an encouraging result.

3.4   Pseudo Labelling

In order to make full use of unlabelled data, we employ a pseudo labelling method. The pseudo labelling method is an unsupervised learning method that uses a model to label unlabelled data, which is called pseudo label. After that we mix the pseudo label data and training data to train the model, so as to improve the result.

In our paper, we choose pre-trained models such as BERT, RoBERTa and ELECTRA, etc. and use the labelled data to fine-tune. Then we predict labels on the test set and get high confidence pseudo label data through voting method. Finally, we integrate the pseudo label data and training data, and train a new model.

3.5   Model Ensemble

According to the models and methods, we use voting to combine the prediction results from multiple models. In event detection task, for every candidate trigger, we count types predicted by multiple models and choose type with the highest number of votes, which is the result of model ensemble. Model ensemble can effectively utilize the advantages of multiple models and obtain prediction results with high confidence. However, there is also the problem of losing correct results in the voting process. To solve this problem, we have added several rules to optimize the existing voting methods. The rules are as follows:

- In order to make the prediction results distribution as close as possible to the distribution of training data, each candidate trigger in training data is counted to obtain the number of event types corresponding to the candidate trigger, and merge the statistical result with the prediction result as the final number of votes.
- After voting, we need to judge the results to ensure that the predicted event types have appeared in training data.
- Count the non-event triggers (negative triggers) that appear frequently in training data. If these candidate triggers are included in the test set, they will be directly set as the non-event triggers, that is, the event types are represented as "None".

4   Experiments

4.1   Dataset

We conduct experiments on CCKS2021 general fine-grained event detection dataset[1], the original text is from Wikipedia. For the English documents and candidate triggers in dataset, we need to identify the event triggers and predict their types. In dataset, the training set contains 2913 documents, the validation

---

[1] https://www.biendata.xyz/competition/ccks_2021_maven/.

set contains 710 documents, and the test set contains 857 documents. It covers 168 general domain event types and contains more than 100,000 event instances. At the same time, event types have a hierarchical structure, which can be basically divided into five main types: Action, Change, Scenario, Sentiment, and Possession, and each main type contains multiple sub-event types.

4.2 Experimental Setup

We tune the parameters based on the Micro F1 score evaluation metric formulated by task 5 of CCKS2021, and finally find the best parameter settings on dataset. Denote A as the number of predicted triggers same as the ground truth, G as the number of predicted triggers, and T as the number of labelled triggers, the precision, recall and Micro F1 score are calculated as follows.

$$precision = \frac{A}{G} \tag{2}$$

$$recall = \frac{A}{T} \tag{3}$$

$$F1 = \frac{2 * precision * recall}{precision + recall} \tag{4}$$

The parameters can be mainly divided into two parts, model parameters and training parameters.

Table 2. Comparison of data augmentation results

Model	P	R	F1
BERT	67.58	69.91	68.72
BERT w/o Data Augmentation	66.27	70.97	68.54
RoBERTa	65.50	71.74	68.48
RoBERTa w/o Data Augmentation	64.93	71.04	67.84
ELECTRA	66.75	71.02	68.82
ELECTRA w/o Data Augmentation	65.45	71.57	68.37
SpanBERT	67.72	70.26	68.96
SpanBERT w/o Data Augmentation	66.22	70.35	68.23
XLNet	65.52	71.98	68.60
XLNet w/o Data Augmentation	64.79	72.14	68.27
UniLM	65.90	72.04	68.83
UniLM w/o Data Augmentation	**67.75**	69.54	68.63
Model Ensemble	67.60	**72.53**	**69.98**

Model Parameters. Due to the model in this paper is based on pre-trained model, we basically follow the parameters of the model, and some parameters are tuned. We apply dropout after the model output with the rate set to 0.5 on XLNet and 0.1 on others. After obtaining the features of each layer, we concatenate the last 4 layers. In terms of sequence length, the XLNet model is set to 180, the RoBERTa model is set to 190, and other models are set to 160. In the data augmentation part, we randomly choose words in the sentence for replacement, the ratio is set to 0.35, and we replace each sentence for 15 times.

Training Parameters. In the training phase, we choose AdamW for optimization and set the learning rate to 1e-5 and 8e-6 for different models. The training epoch is set to 12, batch_size is set to 12, and max_steps is set to 100000. At the same time, in order to improve the training effect, we set warmup_steps to 100. For the data generated by data augmentation and pseudo label data, the sampling ratio is set to 0.4.

Table 3. Comparison of pseudo labelling method results

Model	P	R	F1
BERT	67.89	71.02	69.42
BERT w/o Pseudo Label	66.45	70.77	68.54
RoBERTa	66.88	71.60	69.16
RoBERTa w/o Pseudo Label	66.87	70.62	68.69
ELECTRA	65.78	72.75	69.09
ELECTRA w/o Pseudo Label	66.72	70.64	68.63
SpanBERT	65.51	**73.41**	69.23
SpanBERT w/o Pseudo Label	66.63	71.92	69.17
XLNet	65.94	72.70	69.15
XLNet w/o Pseudo Label	66.96	71.03	68.93
UniLM	65.95	73.12	69.35
UniLM w/o Pseudo Label	67.05	70.86	68.90
Model Ensemble	67.92	71.91	**69.86**
Model Ensemble w/o Pseudo Label	**68.12**	71.37	69.71

4.3   Experimental Results

We fine-tune the pre-trained model with the original training set and the generated data based on pre-trained BERT model(Data Augmentation). "model w/o Data Augmentation" means that the model does not use data generated by data augmentation. According to the results in Table 2, we can find that after using data augmentation, all models have been improved in the F1 score, which verifies the data generated by pre-trained BERT model can enable the model to learn a wider range of features. Furthermore, after using model ensemble, the F1 score reaches 69.98%, resulting in a further improvement. It also verifies the effectiveness of our model ensemble method based on voting and rules for this general fine-grained event detection task.

In addition, we have also conducted research on the effectiveness of pseudo labelling method. "model w/o Pseudo Label" means that the model does not use pseudo label data. According to the results in Table 3, we can find that after using pseudo labelling method, the model has a certain improvement in the F1 score, which also shows the effectiveness of it.

5   Conclusion

In this paper, we propose an event detection scheme based on pre-trained model, combined with data augmentation and pseudo labelling method. Among them, by using pre-trained BERT model for word replacement, the generated data is more effective than other methods, and the pseudo labelling method can make full use of unlabelled data. Furthermore, we have combined multiple models to effectively utilize the advantages of models. The experimental results show that our model achieves significantly performance, the F1 score reaches 69.86% on the test set, ranking the third place in the CCKS2021 general fine-grained event detection competition.

References

1. Ahn, D.: The stages of event extraction. In: Proceedings of the Workshop on Annotating and Reasoning about Time and Events, pp. 1–8 (2006)
2. Chen, Y., Xu, L., Liu, K., Zeng, D., Zhao, J.: Event extraction via dynamic multi-pooling convolutional neural networks. In: Proceedings of the 53rd Annual Meeting of the Association for Computational Linguistics, pp. 167–176. The Association for Computer Linguistics (2015). https://doi.org/10.3115/v1/p15-1017
3. Chen, Y., Yang, H., Liu, K., Zhao, J., Jia, Y.: Collective event detection via a hierarchical and bias tagging networks with gated multi-level attention mechanisms. In: Riloff, E., Chiang, D., Hockenmaier, J., Tsujii, J. (eds.) Proceedings of the 2018 Conference on Empirical Methods in Natural Language Processing, pp. 1267–1276. Association for Computational Linguistics (2018). https://doi.org/10.18653/v1/d18-1158
4. Clark, K., Luong, M., Le, Q.V., Manning, C.D.: ELECTRA: pre-training text encoders as discriminators rather than generators. In: 8th International Conference on Learning Representations. OpenReview.net (2020)
5. Devlin, J., Chang, M., Lee, K., Toutanova, K.: BERT: pre-training of deep bidirectional transformers for language understanding. In: Burstein, J., Doran, C., Solorio, T. (eds.) Proceedings of the 2019 Conference of the North American Chapter of the Association for Computational Linguistics: Human Language Technologies, pp. 4171–4186. Association for Computational Linguistics (2019). https://doi.org/10.18653/v1/n19-1423

6. Ding, N., Li, Z., Liu, Z., Zheng, H., Lin, Z.: Event detection with trigger-aware lattice neural network. In: Inui, K., Jiang, J., Ng, V., Wan, X. (eds.) Proceedings of the 2019 Conference on Empirical Methods in Natural Language Processing and the 9th International Joint Conference on Natural Language Processing, pp. 347–356. Association for Computational Linguistics (2019). https://doi.org/10.18653/v1/D19-1033

7. Dong, L., et al.: Unified language model pre-training for natural language understanding and generation. In: Wallach, H.M., Larochelle, H., Beygelzimer, A., d'Alché-Buc, F., Fox, E.B., Garnett, R. (eds.) Advances in Neural Information Processing Systems 32: Annual Conference on Neural Information Processing Systems 2019, pp. 13042–13054 (2019)

8. Dong, Z., Dong, Q., Hao, C.: Hownet and its computation of meaning. In: COLING 2010, 23rd International Conference on Computational Linguistics, pp. 53–56. Demonstrations Volume (2010)

9. Feng, S.Y., et al.: A survey of data augmentation approaches for NLP. In: Zong, C., Xia, F., Li, W., Navigli, R. (eds.) Findings of the Association for Computational Linguistics. Findings of ACL, vol. ACL/IJCNLP 2021, pp. 968–988. Association for Computational Linguistics (2021). https://doi.org/10.18653/v1/2021.findings-acl.84

10. Hochreiter, S., Schmidhuber, J.: Long short-term memory. Neural Comput. **9**(8), 1735–1780 (1997). https://doi.org/10.1162/neco.1997.9.8.1735

11. Ji, H., Grishman, R.: Refining event extraction through cross-document inference. In: McKeown, K.R., Moore, J.D., Teufel, S., Allan, J., Furui, S. (eds.) ACL 2008, Proceedings of the 46th Annual Meeting of the Association for Computational Linguistics, pp. 254–262. The Association for Computer Linguistics (2008)

12. Joshi, M., Chen, D., Liu, Y., Weld, D.S., Zettlemoyer, L., Levy, O.: Spanbert: Improving pre-training by representing and predicting spans. Trans. Assoc. Comput. Linguistics **8**, 64–77 (2020)

13. Liao, S., Grishman, R.: Using document level cross-event inference to improve event extraction. In: Hajic, J., Carberry, S., Clark, S. (eds.) ACL 2010, Proceedings of the 48th Annual Meeting of the Association for Computational Linguistics, pp. 789–797. The Association for Computer Linguistics (2010)

14. Liu, Y., et al.: Roberta: a robustly optimized BERT pretraining approach. CoRR abs/1907.11692 (2019)

15. Miller, G.A.: Wordnet: a lexical database for English. Commun. ACM **38**(11), 39–41 (1995). https://doi.org/10.1145/219717.219748

16. Walker, C., Strassel, S., Medero, J., Maeda, K.: Ace 2005 multilingual training corpus. Prog. Theor. Phys. Suppl. **110**(110), 261–276 (2006)

17. Wang, X., et al.: MAVEN: a massive general domain event detection dataset. In: Webber, B., Cohn, T., He, Y., Liu, Y. (eds.) Proceedings of the 2020 Conference on Empirical Methods in Natural Language Processing, pp. 1652–1671. Association for Computational Linguistics (2020). https://doi.org/10.18653/v1/2020.emnlp-main.129

18. Yang, Z., Dai, Z., Yang, Y., Carbonell, J.G., Salakhutdinov, R., Le, Q.V.: Xlnet: generalized autoregressive pretraining for language understanding. In: Wallach, H.M., et al. (eds.) Advances in Neural Information Processing Systems 32: Annual Conference on Neural Information Processing Systems 2019, pp. 5754–5764 (2019)

Does BERT Know Which Answer Beyond the Question?

Fei Xia[1,2](✉), Yixuan Weng[1], Maojin Xia[4], Qiang Yu[4], Shizhu He[1,2],
Kang Liu[1,2], Shengping Liu[3], and Jun Zhao[1,2]

[1] National Laboratory of Pattern Recognition Institute of Automation,
Chinese Academy Sciences, Beijing 100190, China
xiafei2020@ia.ac.cn, {shizhu.he,kliu,jzhao}@nlpr.ia.ac.cn
[2] School of Artificial Intelligence, University of Chinese Academy of Sciences,
Beijing 100190, China
[3] Beijing Unisound Information Technology, Beijing 100028, China
liushengping@unisound.com
[4] Qingbo Intelligence Technology Co. Ltd., Hefei, China
{xiamaojin,yuqiang}@gsdata.cn

Abstract. Medical question and answer matching validation (QAMV)
aims to construct an intelligent medical question answering classification
system, which can use massive medical information content to quickly
meet user needs and ensure the accuracy and authority of the content.
This paper presents our proposed framework for the Chinese QAMV
organized by the 2021 China conference on knowledge graph and semantic computing (CCKS) competition, which requires correct classification
of whether the answer can satisfy the related question. After the prelim-
inary experiment, we analyzed the bad cases in-depth and found hard
instances and insufficient model generalization capabilities. In order to
solve these problems, we have proposed a series of innovative strategies,
including five categories of methods: 1) Four different adversarial training methods 2) Hard instances identification and multi-round training
methods 3) Target instances constructed by similarity 4) Validation set
retraining with a small learning rate 5) Medical word vector combined
with Easy Data Augmentation (EDA) method for text data augmentation. Our innovative approach has improved by an average of 1.164%
compared to the baseline. The experiment fully shows that our innovative method is very effective. The method we proposed won the CCKS
competition and was significantly ahead of the second opponent (close to
1%) in the final, showing extremely high practicality and effectiveness.

Keywords: Question and answer · Adversarial learning · Data
augmentation

F. Xia and Y. Weng—These authors contributed equally to the work.

B. Qin et al. (Eds.): CCKS 2021, CCIS 1553, pp. 69–81, 2022.
https://doi.org/10.1007/978-981-19-0713-5_9

1   Introduction

With the development of science and technology and economic progress, people are paying more and more attention to health issues, and the popularization of medical science information has also been recognized and valued by the state and society. Internet technology is changing with each passing day, and new content forms such as graphics, question answering, short videos, and live broadcasts are emerging one after another. How to use the massive medical information content to quickly meet user needs and ensure the accuracy and authority of the content is a very important topic.

As a result, building an intelligent medical question answering (QA) system is beneficial to improving patients' satisfaction and reducing the burden on doctors. To promote the research on the quality of Chinese medical question answering, the 15th China Conference on Knowledge Graph and Semantic Computing (CCKS 2021) sets Task 12 for Medical question and answer matching validation (QAMV), Where requires participants to accurately identify answers beyond the question (hereinafter referred to as the non-ideal answer) in the medical field. However, the most challenging is that there are few non-ideal answers, and many of them are difficult to understand for the model. The non-ideal answer refers to answer A cannot satisfy the query Q. In the content of medical science popularization, there are generally two forms of non-ideal questions as shown in Fig. 1. One is answer A is entirely unrelated to question Q and cannot answer the question asked,the other is that answer A is related to question Q, but the answer is in the wrong direction.

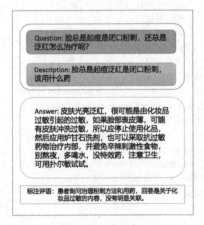
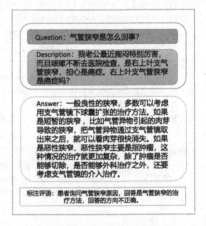

Type1-Unrelated answer   **Type2- Relevant but the wrong-direction answer**

Fig. 1. Two types of non-ideal answers.

After the baseline experiment, we analyzed the bad cases in-depth and found hard instances and insufficient model generalization capabilities. In order to solve these problems, we have proposed a series of innovative strategies, including five categories of methods:

- Four different adversarial training methods. We researched and compared FGM [9], PGD [7], gradient loss [10], and R-Drop [6]. We also experimented with the combination of FGM and R-Drop and delayed adversarial training. This method improves by 1.64% relative to the baseline.
- Hard instances identification and multi-round training methods. We use external data combined with the pseudo-label [5] method to train a selection model for selecting error-prone and low-confidence instances. After that, we carry out multiple rounds of retraining on selected hard instances according to the ideas of curriculum learning [1]. This method improves by 1.01% relative to the baseline.
- Target instances constructed by similarity. We use the similarity algorithm edit distance [13] to augmented the target instances. This method improves by 0.99% relative to the baseline.
- Validation set retraining with a small learning rate. To make full use of the data, we conducted many experiments on the validation set. Experiments show that retraining the validation set with a small learning rate(2.00E-06) can improve the baseline (0.99%).
- Medical word vector combined with Easy Data Augmentation (EDA) [12] method for text data augmentation. We use medical word vectors combined with EDA for text data augmentation, using RS (replace synonymous medical words), RR (replace random words), SR (swap sentences randomly), ID (insert and delete words randomly). This method improves by 1.19% relative to the baseline.

2   Method

In this section, we will first illustrate the structure of our basic framework. After that, we analyzed the error instances and explored the possible causes. Finally, to solve these problems, we proposed a series of innovative strategies, which are also the critical parts of this article, and we will explain the details of each component.

2.1   Baseline Model

Our baseline model is shown in Fig. 2. We connect the question, description, and answer with [SEP] as the model's input, and the output is the 0/1 label. We have tried various Chinese pre-trained models, including BERT-wwm [3], BERT-wwm-ext [2], chinese-roberta-wwm-ext [2], MacBERT [2] etc. Based on the experimental results, we used MacBERT as the baseline pre-training model. We use the five-fold stratified sampling method to divide the training set and the validation set and measure whether the current parameters are good enough according to the model's performance on different data. We also used an adversarial training [4] method to perturb the input data. (Specifically, we tried the

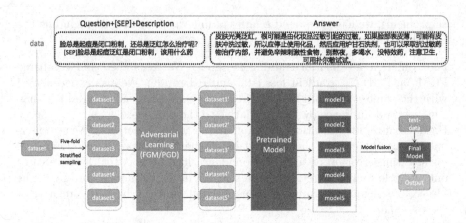

Fig. 2. Input and baseline.

two standard ways of FGM and PGD) Our purpose is to enhance the generalization ability of the model for correct classification. At the same time, this is equivalent to training five different models. We use a weighted model fusion method to fuse these five models into the final model and predict the label of the test set data.

2.2   Analysis of Bad Cases

To understand the problems of the current model and the direction of improvement, we analyzed and studied the samples of the current baseline model that are incorrectly predicted. The experiment uses 35,000 instances for training and 5,000 data for prediction. There are 317 prediction errors in the tested 5k samples, of which 160 are incorrectly predicted as an unanswered question (label 1), and 157 are incorrectly predicted as a standard question and answer (label 0).

After analysis, we found that there are mainly the following questions:

1) Question: The question is not a question but a description of a phenomenon or unclear question.
2) Description: Description and question are contradictory.
3) Answer: The answer does not respond to the question positively or is not clear. It requires a specific reasoning ability to judge whether it is an ideal answer.

Questions 1 and 2 are the problems of the data itself, and question 3 is the problem of insufficient model capabilities. Therefore, we focus on reducing the impact of erroneous data and improving the model's generalisation ability so that the model can classify complex samples more accurately.

It is worth noting that although the classification effect of the model we tested locally is perfect, there is still a particular gap (5%–10%) between the classification effect of the online model and the local model. We speculate that the generalization ability of the current model may not be strong enough. Or there is a certain amount of complex samples in online data.

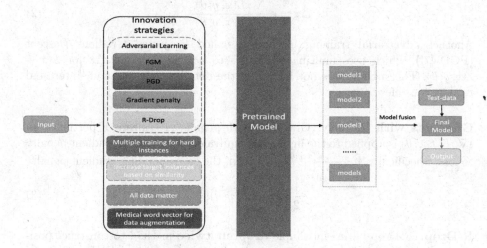

Fig. 3. The overall framework of the integration of innovation strategies.

3   Innovation Strategies

This section mainly introduces our innovation strategies. The overall framework is shown in Fig. 3. Each module has a high degree of independence and can be used alone or in any combination. We have designed several different methods for data and model problems. After our experiments, these strategies are very effective. We will introduce each innovation module in detail in the following.

3.1   Adversarial Training for Instances Augmentation

In recent years, with the increasing development and implementation of deep learning, adversarial training have also received more and more attention. In NLP, adversarial training is more used as a regularization method to improve the generalization ability[1] of the model.

FGM/PGD. The common method in adversarial training is the Fast Gradient Method (FGM [9]). The idea of FGM is straightforward. Increasing the loss is to increase the gradient so that we can take

$$\Delta x = \epsilon \nabla_x L(x, y; \theta) \tag{1}$$

Where x represents the input, y represents the label, θ is the model parameter, $L(x, y; \theta)$ is the loss of a single sample, Δx is the anti-disturbance.

---

[1] https://spaces.ac.cn/archives/7234.

Of course, to prevent Δx from being too large, it is usually necessary to standardize $\nabla_x L(x, y; \theta)$. The more common way is

$$\Delta x = \epsilon \frac{\nabla_x L(x, y; \theta)}{\|\nabla_x L(x, y; \theta)\|} \tag{2}$$

Another adversarial training method is called Projected Gradient Descent (PGD [7]), which uses multiple iterations to achieve a larger Δx for $L(x + \Delta x, y; \theta)$. This article does not introduce the details of the method. Interested readers can refer to it.

Gradients with Penalty. Gradients with penalty [10] means if perturbation $\epsilon \nabla_x L(x, y; \theta)$ is applied to the input, it is equivalent to adding a gradient penalty to loss. Specifically, if $\epsilon \frac{\nabla_x L(x, y; \theta)}{\|\nabla_x L(x, y; \theta)\|}$ is added, the corresponding gradient penalty is

$$\frac{1}{2} \epsilon \|\nabla_x L(x, y; \theta)\|^2 \tag{3}$$

R-Drop. R-Drop [6] uses a simple **dropout twice** method to construct positive samples for comparative learning, significantly improving the experimental results in supervised tasks. Figure 4 shows the framework of RDrop.

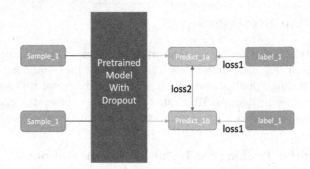

Fig. 4. Schematic diagram of method RDrop.

Specifically, the training data is $\{x_i, y_i\}_{i=1}^n$, and the model is $P_\theta(y \mid x)$. The loss of R-Drop is divided into two parts, one part is conventional cross entropy:

$$\mathcal{L}_i^{(CE)} = -\log P_\theta^{(1)}(y_i \mid x_i) - \log P_\theta^{(2)}(y_i \mid x_i) \tag{4}$$

The other part is the symmetric KL divergence between the two models. It hopes that the output of different Dropout models is as consistent as possible:

$$\mathcal{L}_i^{(KL)} = \frac{1}{2} \left[KL \left(P_\theta^{(2)}(y \mid x_i) \| P_\theta^{(1)}(y \mid x_i) \right) + KL \left(P_\theta^{(1)}(y \mid x_i) \| P_\theta^{(2)}(y \mid x_i) \right) \right]$$

The final loss is the weighted sum of the two losses:

$$\mathcal{L}_i = \mathcal{L}_i^{(CE)} + \alpha \mathcal{L}_i^{(KL)} \tag{5}$$

3.2 Multiple Training for Error-Prone and Difficult Instances

In the bad case study, we found that many examples are hard and often incorrectly predicted by the model. We used the Chinese medical dialogue dataset[2] to find this part of the examples. First, we used the baseline model to pseudo-label the Chinese medical dialogue dataset. Then we use this part of pseudo-label [5] data to train a selection model for selecting error-prone and challenging samples. We use model to predict the original labeled training set and record the incorrect and low-confidence data as error-prone and complex samples. After that, we will add this part of the data in each training process and let the model train on this data multiple times. We found that this method can enhance the model's classification accuracy for complex samples (Fig. 5).

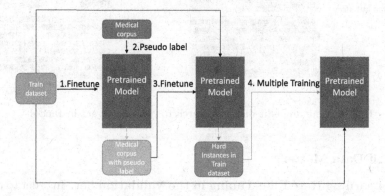

Fig. 5. Multiple training for error-prone and difficult instances.

3.3 Minimum Edit Distance Search to Increase Target Instances

In order to increase the number of samples with label 1, we also manually constructed the data. After analyzing the data, we found that even if the two questions are very similar, the corresponding answer is very different. In short, in the standard question and answer (label 0), replace the question with another very similar question, and the answer will be a non-ideal answer (label 1). Moreover, samples constructed in this way are generally more complex, which helps the model learn from hard samples. So we first find out the most similar set of answers in the training set and exchange the answers with each other, which constitutes two sets of answer data. As for measuring similarity, we first wanted to use SimBERT [11] to find the two most similar sentences, but because simBERT takes much time, we finally used the classic edit distance [13] method in measuring similarity to achieve this goal. Its performance is also excellent (Fig. 6).

---

[2] https://github.com/GanjinZero/awesome_Chinese_medical_NLP.

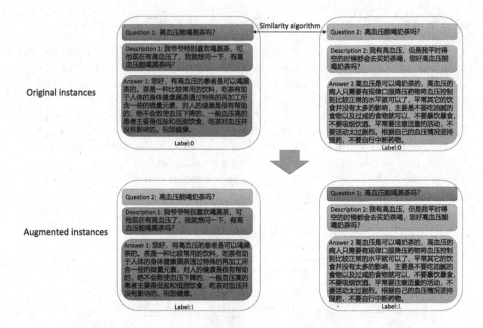

Fig. 6. Minimum edit distance search to increase target instances.

3.4 All Data Matter

Small Learning Rate Fine-Tuning in the Validation Set. In order to make full use of the value of data, we also thought of validation set data. To measure the effect of model classification, we divide the original data into a training set and a validation set. After every epoch training, we will verify its performance on the validation set, and finally, we choose the model that performs best on the validation set. The model has not seen these validation set data during the training phase, so it may be helpful if retrained. At first, let the currently trained optimal model train another round on the validation set, but there is no improvement in the expected effect. Instead, the model reduces part of the classification ability due to this part of the addition. We analyze that it may have the following reasons: 1. With the catastrophic forgetting [8] of deep learning, the model may forget the memory as training increases. 2. The distribution of the verification set may be different. The model may have learned some features, but its generalization ability may be weakened. Therefore, we tried to reduce the learning rate and make the model learn less on these unseen data. Finally, the experiment showed that this method is very significant. This method is practical and straightforward and can be used in any task that uses deep learning. It has a general improvement. We think it is one of the powerful innovations of this experiment.

Testset A Data. In the final test phase, we also used the test data from the A test phase. Considering our excellent performance in the A test phase and high accuracy, we believe that this part of the pseudo-label data with high accuracy is also valuable. So we add this part of the data to the model training, and use the trained model to predict the results. Unsurprisingly, our results have improved again, which proves that it is indeed effective. All data matter (Fig. 7).

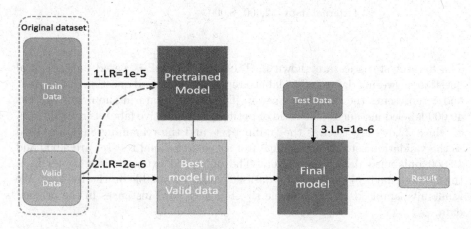

Fig. 7. Small learning rate fine-tuning in the validation set.

3.5   Medical Word Vector for Data Augmentation

In the research process, we fully realized the role of data, so we also tried other data enhancement methods. We used the medical word vector trained by ourselves and combined it with the classic text data augmentation method EDA [12]. Specifically, we replaced the medical similar word vector and performed operations such as random exchange of sentences, random deletion, and insertion of words. However, we think replacing similar words will likely cause the original normal standard question and answer to become non-ideal (the experiment also reflects this). So when using similar words to replace, we also record the corresponding data label as 1. This method can further improve the classification effect of our model. However, due to limited time, we have not been able to conduct a more in-depth study. We believe that the value of this medical word vector is far more than that, and we will further study its use scenarios in the future.

4   Experiments

In this section, we will introduce the dataset, evaluation, implementation and results of the experiments.

4.1 Dataset

Table 1. Statistics of dataset.

	Train	Dev	Test A	Test B
Original data	32,000	8,000	5,000	10,000
External data	32,000	8,000	–	–

The dataset statistics are shown in Table 1. This task is based on a medical question answering dataset. The label 0 represents standard question and answer, and 1 represents the non-ideal answer. The original data in the first stage has 40,000 labeled instances (the ratio of positive and negative labels is roughly 1:2), of which 32,000 are used as the training set, and the remaining 8,000 are used as the validation set. The first stage test set and the final test set are 5,000 and 10,000 unlabeled data, respectively. The unlabeled external data comes from the Chinese medical conversation dataset publicly available on the Internet. We randomly sample data of the same size to select hard instances in the original data.

4.2 Evaluation

This task uses precision (Precision, P), recall (Recall, R), and F1 value (F1-measure, F1) to evaluate the recognition effect of the non-ideal answer (using F1 value as the ranking basis).

4.3 Results

In this Section, we will show our experimental results and online results under various methods.

Experimental Results on the Baseline. To choose a model suitable for this task, we compared 4 Chinese pre-training models. As shown in Table 2, we conducted baseline experiments, and the Mac-BERT-large [2] model has the best performance (F1:89.61). At the same time, to verify the role of adversarial training, we also compared the effect of whether to add FGM [9]/PGD [7]. The results show that an average of 0.58% improves the classification effect of the model after FGM/PGD, and the Mac-BERT-large model is also the best one. Therefore, we finally choose it as our baseline backbone and further research and improve the adversarial training in the follow-up innovation strategy.

Experimental Results of Innovative Strategies
Adversarial Training. As is shown in the Table 3, we further studied the adversarial training and compared the experimental results of FGM [9]/PGD [7], gradient penalty [10], R-Drop [6], and the combination of FGM and R-Drop. The

Table 2. Results of different pre-trained models and with or without FGM/PGD on the baseline.

Model	No-FGM/PGD	FGM/PGD
BERT-wwm	89.19	90.02 (+0.83)
BERT-wwm-ext	89.59	90.2 (+0.61)
Chinese-roberta-wwm-ext	89.33	89.22 (−0.11)
Mac-BERT-large	**89.61**	**90.59 (+0.98)**
Average	89.43	90.01 (+0.58)

results show that adversarial training is beneficial for the current task. Among them, the use of FGM alone and the combination of FGM and R-Drop have improved by nearly 1% compared to the baseline. In addition, we consider that the model may not be fully trained in the early stage, so we adopt a delay strategy. Regular training in the early stage and adversarial training only in the later stage. The delayed confrontation strategy has also further improved the model classification performance, which is 1.64% higher than the baseline and 0.66% higher than the previous best performance.

Table 3. Results of adversarial training.

Baseline	FGM	gradient penalty	R-Drop	FGM&R-Drop	delay FGM&R-Drop
89.61	90.59	90.44	89.86	90.56	**91.25**

Multiple Training for Hard Instances and Increase Target Instances. We use model prediction errors and low-confidence data as hard instances to add to training and adjust the proportion and total data for comparison. As shown in Table 4, when the wrong prediction and low-confidence instances each account for 50%, the result is the best, 90.62%, which is an increase of 1.01% compared to the baseline. We adopt this ratio in subsequent experiments. We also experimented with minimizing the edit distance [13] to amplify the target example. The improvement effect is almost the same as the best effect of multiple training for hard instances.

Table 4. Multiple training for hard instances and increase target instances.

Baseline	1/2 predicted wrong and 1/2 low confidence (4000)			All predicted wrong (4000)	All low confidence (4000)	Edit distance
	add (1/3) 1333	add (2/3) 2666	add (3/3) 4000			
89.61	90.17	90.52	**90.62**	90.36	90.15	**90.6**

Table 5. Retraining results with different small learning rates on the validation set.

Best model	Small learning rate					
	2.00E-04	2.00E-05	5.00E-06	2.00E-06	8.00E-07	2.00E-07
90.21	67.67	90.32	90.58	**90.6**	90.32	90.34

Retraining on Validation Set with Small Learning Rate. To fully use the data, we use the validation set to retrain with a small learning rate. As shown in Table 5, when using the 2.00E-06 learning rate, the result is 0.39% better than the baseline.

Medical Word Vector for Easy Data Augmentation (MEDA). We use medical word vectors combined with EDA for text data augmentation, using RS (replace synonymous medical words), RR (replace random words), SR (swap sentences randomly), ID (insert and delete words randomly). We found that the above operations may cause label changes during the experiment, so we also compared the observed effects after changing the labels. As shown in Table 6, the use of RR operation is 0.38% higher than the baseline. We found that changes to the text may indeed cause label changes.

Table 6. Results of using medical word vector for data augmentation.

	Original	RS	RR	SR	ID
Label unchanged	90.42	90.2	–	90.15	90.72
Change label to 1	–	90.5	**90.8**	90.41	90.61

We compared the innovation methods, and the results are shown in Table 7. The experimental results show that our functions are practical and have an average improvement of 1.164% compared to the baseline. We also used a combination of all the strategies, and the result was 2.11% better than baseline, much better than using a single method. You can try any variety of these methods.

Table 7. Results of different innovation methods.

Baseline	Adversarial	Hard instances	Edit distance	Validation retrain	MEDA	All
89.61	91.25 (+1.64)	90.62 (+1.01)	90.6 (+0.99)	90.6 (+0.99)	90.8 (+1.19)	91.72 (+2.11)

5 Conclusion

In this paper, we conducted a deep analysis of instances and found that there are problems such as complex instances and insufficient model generalization capabilities. We propose an innovative strategy to solve these problems, which consists of five parts: 1) Four different adversarial training methods 2) Complex instances recognition model and multi-round training methods 3) Target examples constructed by similarity 4) The validation set small learning rate retraining 5) Medical word vector combined with EDA method for text data amplification. We achieved the best results in the CCKS competition, which proved the effectiveness and practicality of our proposed method. In the future, we will consider using medical word vectors for data amplification and try different fusion methods further to improve the accuracy and quality of the generated responses.

References

1. Bengio, Y., Louradour, J., Collobert, R., Weston, J.: Curriculum learning. In: Proceedings of the 26th Annual International Conference on Machine Learning, pp. 41–48 (2009)
2. Cui, Y., Che, W., Liu, T., Qin, B., Wang, S., Hu, G.: Revisiting pre-trained models for Chinese natural language processing. In: Proceedings of the 2020 Conference on Empirical Methods in Natural Language Processing: Findings, pp. 657–668. Association for Computational Linguistics, Online, November 2020. https://www.aclweb.org/anthology/2020.findings-emnlp.58
3. Cui, Y., et al.: Pre-training with whole word masking for Chinese Bert. arXiv preprint arXiv:1906.08101 (2019)
4. Ganin, Y., et al.: Domain-adversarial training of neural networks. J. Mach. Learn. Res. 17(1), 1–35 (2016)
5. Lee, D.H., et al.: Pseudo-label: the simple and efficient semi-supervised learning method for deep neural networks. In: Workshop on Challenges in Representation Learning, ICML, vol. 3, p. 896 (2013)
6. Liang, X., et al.: R-drop: regularized dropout for neural networks. arXiv preprint arXiv:2106.14448 (2021)
7. Madry, A., Makelov, A., Schmidt, L., Tsipras, D., Vladu, A.: Towards deep learning models resistant to adversarial attacks. arXiv preprint arXiv:1706.06083 (2017)
8. McCloskey, M., Cohen, N.J.: Catastrophic interference in connectionist networks: the sequential learning problem. In: Psychology of Learning and Motivation, vol. 24, pp. 109–165. Elsevier (1989)
9. Miyato, T., Dai, A.M., Goodfellow, I.: Adversarial training methods for semi-supervised text classification. arXiv preprint arXiv:1605.07725 (2016)
10. Ross, A.S., Doshi-Velez, F.: Improving the adversarial robustness and interpretability of deep neural networks by regularizing their input gradients. In: Thirty-Second AAAI Conference on Artificial Intelligence (2018)
11. Su, J.: Simbert: integrating retrieval and generation into bert. Technical report (2020). https://github.com/ZhuiyiTechnology/simbert
12. Wei, J., Zou, K.: Eda: easy data augmentation techniques for boosting performance on text classification tasks. ArXiv:abs/1901.11196 (2019)
13. Yujian, L., Bo, L.: A normalized levenshtein distance metric. IEEE Trans. Pattern Anal. Mach. Intell. 29(6), 1091–1095 (2007)

End-to-End Pre-trained Dialogue System for Automatic Diagnosis

Yuan Wang[1,2(✉)], Zekun Li[1], Leilei Zeng[1], and Tingting Zhao[1]

[1] College of Artificial Intelligence, Tianjin University of Science and Technology,
Tianjin 300457, China
wangyuan23@tust.edu.cn
[2] Population and Precision Health Care, Ltd., Tianjin 300000, China

Abstract. With the development of medical technology, Chinese medical resources are extremely scarce. At this necessary time, the development of dialogue agents to interact with patients and provide clinical advice has attracted more and more attention. In the task of generative medical dialogue, the end-to-end method is often used to establish the model. However, traditional end-to-end models often generate deficient relevance to medical dialogue. Towards this end, we propose to integrate medical information into initial pre-trained model and use the division of sentence based on "words and expressions" to improve the accuracy of medical entity recall, which will make the model have a deeper understanding of medical field. Finally, we use the Chinese medical dialogue MedDG [1] to fine-tune the model, so that the model can give the reply to the doctor's clinical inquiry for the disease content from the patient. The experimental results show that our framework achieves higher accuracy in disease diagnosis, which won the fourth place in the 2021 medical dialogue generation task containing Chinese.

Keywords: Dialog generation · Online consultation · Pre-trained model

1 Introduction

In recent years, the imbalance between the aging of population and the scarcity of medical staff have become increasingly prominent. Medical consultation is one of the important links and the main factor of the efficiency bottleneck of medical practice.

In order to improve the efficiency of diagnosis, artificial intelligence technology is used to reduce the burden of doctors. Industrial community often adopts popular pipeline and end-to-end methods to deal with the generation of medical dialogue. The pipeline mode mainly involves domain identification, intention identification and the filling of slot values. However, in this modular design framework, each module needs to be trained separately, which makes the downstream tasks vulnerably to the impact of early modules, making the performance of the whole system unsteadily owing to the accumulated errors [2]. The traditional methods of using end-to-end methods to deal with dialog generation tasks include RNN [3], LSTM [4] and so on. RNN is prone to gradient disappearance or gradient explosion, which is often insufficient for processing

© Springer Nature Singapore Pte Ltd. 2022
B. Qin et al. (Eds.): CCKS 2021, CCIS 1553, pp. 82–91, 2022.
https://doi.org/10.1007/978-981-19-0713-5_10

long text sequences. In order to solve this problem, LSTM uses the valve mechanism to alleviate the disadvantages in a certain extent. However, based on the interdependence of the results of time step, even in BiLSTM. There are still defects in using context information. The key to deal with the medical dialogue task in an end-to-end way is to obtain a large number of clinical corpus, but these data are private, and the open corpus dialogue is also very rare. For the data in the Chinese dialogue, please refer to the MedDG, which involves 12 diseases relatively to gastroenterology, including more than 17000 dialogues and 380000 sentences.

This paper use the pre-trained model of T5 based on attention mechanism as the basic template to make full use of context information. So better results can be achieved by using less label data. In order to make T5 model understand medical texts more deeply, we use the medical dialogue of MedDialog [5] to pre-training the model. At the same time, in order to recall as many medical entities as possible in the doctor's reply, we modify the tokenizer of T5. Firstly, common medical entities are added to its dictionary set, and then word segmentation based on "words and expressions" is used to segment sentences. Each data set of medical dialogue is composed of multiple rounds of dialogue between doctors and patients, each data set is marked with medical entity. Such as symptoms, frequency, drugs and so on, as shown in Table 1. In order to make the format of data conform entered style (dialogue, result) of the model, where dialogue is the input of model and result is the label of model. We preprocess the original data set

Table 1. Example of training data

Self-report
胃部不适，第一天有痛感，后面就是胀，不拉肚子，请问是什么原（男，39 岁）
Stomach discomfort, pain on the first day, followed by swelling and no diarrhea. What is the reason(male, 39 years old)
症状：腹痛，腹胀
Symptoms: abdominal pain, abdominal distension

Conversation
Doctor:您好，您的症状有多久了呢？ 属性：时常
Hello, how long have you had symptoms? Attribute: time
Doctor:平时有没有反酸嗳气，大便情况怎么样？ 属性：打嗝，反流
Do you have acid regurgitation and belching at ordinary times?
How about the stool? Properties: hiccup, reflux
Patient:反酸不明显，大便正常。属性：反酸
The acid reflux is not obvious, and the stool is normal.
Properties: reflux
Doctor:您这属于消化不良造成的，建议口服奥美拉唑进行治疗。 属性：消化不良，奥美拉唑
This is caused by indigestion. It is recommended to take oral omeprazole for treatment.
Properties: dyspepsia, omeprazole
...

so that the result is the doctor's reply. The "dialogue" is the multiple rounds of dialogue between the doctor and patient before the doctor replies to the "result" (Fig. 2).

The content of this paper can be summarized as follows: the second section introduces the existing problems and solutions in the traditional dialogue generation task, the third section introduces the models used in this task, the fourth section selects different models to display the experimental results, and the fifth section summarizes the overall framework.

2 Related Work

The natural language understanding of medical dialogue has been extensively studied in recent years. Its main work is to reply the symptoms of future patients through the historical dialogue between doctors and patients. [6] and Automatic phenotype identification using electronic health records (EHR) has been a rising topic in recent years [7]. Because each EMR contains several data types, including personal information, diagnostic examination, physical characteristics. The statistics of these data need to be accumulated according to the clinical diagnostic procedure. Therefore, it is very expensive to collect EHRs for different diseases. How to collect the information from patient automatically remains the challenge for automatic diagnosis. Wei et al. (2018) first use reinforcement learning (RL) to extract symptoms as actions for disease diagnosis. [8] Liao et al. (2020) use a hierarchical RL model to alleviate the large action space problem. [9] Although the above strategies have achieved good results in symptom recognition and disease diagnosis according to specific symptoms, there are still deficiencies in the generation of fluent and complete dialogue. In the process of dealing with medical dialogue. Liu et al. (2020) propose a medical dialogue generation system framework with entity prediction strategy. The framework is composed of entity prediction module and dialogue generation module. The entity prediction module is used to predict the medical entities contained in the training data reply to guide the model to generate relevant medical entities. The dialogue generation module is used to complete the generation of medical dialogue, and the framework will produce the problem of error accumulation between different modules. Budzianowski et al. (2019) used the pre-trained GPT-2 model for task-based dialogue tasks [10], but based on the greedy strategy of generating replies and the lack of deep understanding of the input content at the coding end, which are slightly insufficient, and often generate general and meaningless replies such as "uh huh". By constructing "cluster search", this paper selects the comprehensive maximization results from the possibility of multiple responses.

3 Model

3.1 Task Definition

The purpose of the medical dialogue system is to generate a doctor response that is consistent with the context and has practically medical significance according to the dialogue history of doctors and patients, particularly emphasis is placed on the correct description and medical diagnostic interpretation of the associated medical entities. In the task, we mainly focus on the statement generation of response. Formally, given the dialogue history $X = <x_1, x_2,..., x_n>$ between doctors and patients, where $x_1 - x_{n-1}$ is a sentence of doctors or patients, and x_n is the sentence of patients. Each sentence may contain various medical entities, such as symptoms, duration, drugs, etc. For the next sentence, the doctor's reply Y is the diseased treatment in consideration of the patient's comprehensive symptoms. The response should include as many medical entities as possible and comply with the medical rules of the corresponding symptoms.

3.2 T5-Medicine Model

The medical dialogue generation adopts an end-to-end way. The technology based on deep learning usually does not rely on specific templates, but carries out the dialogue according to the characteristic relationship of language from a large number of corpora, which emphasizes the positional relationship between words, which is also consistent with human cognition of natural language. That is, when people do text processing, they will consider it macroscopically in combination with the context. At the input end, the historical dialogue is used as the input sequence, which includes the symptoms of the patient and the doctor's inquiry. Firstly, the historical dialogue is transformed into a digital vector, and the final coding vector of the input sequence is obtained through the operation of self-attention mechanism and forward neural network at the encoder end of the model. At the decoder end, the doctor's reply sequence is the result content of the encoder end successively through the operation of masked self-attention mechanism, self-attention mechanism, forward neural network and masked matrix. The sequence is obtained by the model considering the patient's problems comprehensively. It should include as many corresponding medical entities as possible and the content should comply with the medical reply. Its basic mathematical principle is maximum likelihood estimation method, such as formula (1). The overall model framework is shown in Fig. 1:

$$P(y|x) = P(y_1, y_2, \ldots, y_n|x) = P(y_1|x)P(y_2|x,y_1)\ldots P(y_n|x, y_1, \ldots, y_{n-1})$$
$$= \prod_{i=1}^{n-1} P(y|x, y_{1:i}) \tag{1}$$

where x is the medical input content, y is the overall output content, and y_i is the output of each time step, $y_{1:i}$ is the output of the previous part of i.

In the course of processing the code of input sequence. Firstly, the input sequence is preliminarily segmented, the embedded vector of the sequence is constructed by the relative position of the word in the dictionary, and the position vector of the sequence is obtained by sinusoidal position coding. The introduction of position vector is to capture a context relationship between words and effectively deal with the phenomenon of polysemy. Then the two vectors are superimposed and summed to obtain the word vector of the sequence.

There are multi-layer encoder and multi-layer decoder in T5 model, each encoder and decoder layer consist of 12 blocks, and the attention mechanism has 12 headers in each block. In order to make the model learn and understand medical entities more deeply, this paper modifies the original word segmentation based on "word" to word segmentation based on "words and expressions". In order to strengthen the sensitivity of the model to medical content, a large number of medical corpus are put into the model to train, so as to form the T5-medicine.

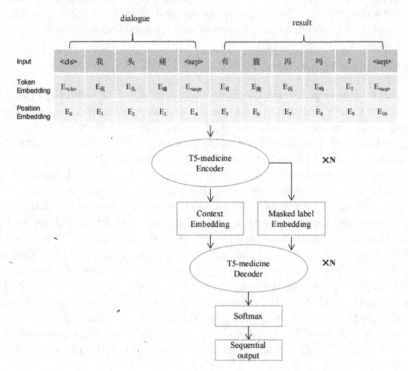

Fig. 1. T5-medicine framework for model operation

3.3   Word Segmentation Based on "Words and Expressions"

For the word segmentation of input sequence, this paper adopts the word segmentation method based on "words and expressions". The specific method is to add 160 common entities for the model dictionary set, which contains common Chinese words, Then, "Jieba" (word segmentation tool) is used to segment the input sequence1, thus, the list of word segmentation L is obtained, and each word or words and expressions 2 in L is traversed. If the word or words and expressions is in the dictionary set, the result is added to the candidate list R, otherwise we will repeat 1. The final candidate list R is the word segmentation result. The reasons for adopting words and expressions are as follows:

Because Chinese is different from English in expression, English segmentation unit is a word and there are spaces between words, However, Chinese naturally does not have these characteristics. Chinese includes single word, double words and idioms. Therefore, there are various differences in the division process. Compared with "word granularity" segmentation. Firstly, the sequence obtained by "words and expressions" segmentation will be shorter and the processing speed will be faster, Secondly, exposure bias can be alleviated during the generation of dialogue reply, Finally, the uncertainty of the obtained word is decreased, which reduces the complexity of the model.

3.4 Model Training

In order to make the model better conform to the Chinese context and have a deeper understanding of the text in the medical field. Firstly, the medical corpus MedDialog is used to pre-training the model, and then the preprocessed MedDG is used to fine-tune the downstream model to achieve the best effect.

In the process of pre-training the model with MedDialog, each data in MedDialog is a complete medical dialogue. The method of completing dialogue training is different from the previous self-supervised training in which random mask is used to fill in the blanks, instead, a quarter of the paragraph is randomly extracted as the output, and the remaining three quarters are spliced in sequence as the input to predict the output. The advantage is that it can promote the model to understand the whole document and pay more attention to the generation of complete sentences. So as to reduce the migration cost and make it closer to downstream tasks.

Based on the weight of the pre-trained parameters of the medical corpus, the processed MedDG is used as the initial training data. The cross entropy is used as the loss function, the optimizer uses Adam and sets the learning rate to $2e - 5$, so as to fine-tune the model with supervised learning.

4 Experiments

4.1 Dataset

In the process of building the medical dialogue model, this paper uses the data of MedDialog as a pre-trained data set, including 3.4 million complete Chinese dialogues between doctors and patients, There are 13 million paragraphs in total, and each dialogue starts from describing the status of patient and past medical history, including current disease duration, drug treatment, etc. Then, fine-tuning the downstream model by the MedDG. This paper connects each data into a complete conversation, and then preprocesses the data, so as to convert 14836 conversation data into 73000. There are 160 entity items, including 12 diseases, 62 symptoms, 4 attributes, 20 examinations and 62 drugs. For training data statistics, the maximum length, minimum length and average length of dialogue can be obtained in Table 2.

4.2 Data Preprocessing

Because the evaluation involves the generation of entities, we filter out the sentences without entities in the doctor's reply. Here, we extract the id field (Doctor/Patient) of each complete conversation and the conversation content of the corresponding person, which are spliced in sequence. We convert the format of data to (dialogue, result). The

Table 2. The statistic of fine-tuning data

Type	Max.tokens	Min.tokens	Mean.tokens
Dialogue	2449	7	281
Result	1539	3	25

"result" is the doctor's reply, and the "dialogue" is multiple rounds of dialogue between the doctor and patient before the doctor replies to the "result", Fig. 2 is the example of preprocessing result.

4.3 Evaluation

In the verification phase of medical dialogue generation task, we use BLEU-AVE [11] to measure the similarity between the model generated sentences and the text provided by doctors. This evaluation mainly considers the average similarity of one, two, three and four tuples at the character level. The entity recall rate F1 [12] is used to measure the accuracy of entities involved in model generation statements.

4.4 Configuration

This paper compares the traditional RNN, MT5-base, GPT-2 and T5-medicine. The input and output dimensions of RNN are set to 300, the training batch is set to 12, the initial learning rate is set to 0.001, and the optimizer is set to random gradient descent method. For MT5, we follow the original parameter to fine-tune the model. We set the maximum input dimension to 512, the maximum output dimension to 100, the training batch to 4, and the initial learning rate to e − 4. In the process of fine-tuning T5-medicine, we set the maximum input dimension to 465, the maximum output dimension to 100, the learning rate to 2e − 5, and the model optimizer to Adam.

4.5 Result

Experiments show that compared with other models, the logic and correctness of generated content of RNN based model are general, then Entity-F1 and BLEU-AVE are significantly reduced. The reason may be that the length of text processed by RNN is limited and the training process is not easy to converge, so the optimal weight parameters can not be reached. For the comparison between MT5 and T5-medicine, we find that the evaluation indexes of MT5 are generally lower than those of T5-medicine. The reason for this result is that the parameters of MT5 are trained by multilingual corpus (Table 3 shows the generation results of different models for a conversation). Therefore, they tend to generate unrelated responses to the medical field. The parameters of T5-medicine have a deeper understanding of medical content after pre-training of medical articles. Compared with T5-medicine model, GPT-2 has less training corpus and lacks encoder, so it can not fully learn the input content, so the result will be slightly worse. The evaluation results are shown in Table 4:

Table 3. Model evaluation

Model	Entity-F1	BLEU-AVE
RNN	0.1137	0.0502
GPT-2	0.2043	0.1011
MT5-base	0.2177	0.0932
T5-medicine	**0.2644**	**0.1268**

Table 4. Prediction results of different models on the same training data

dialogue	Model Response
患者：总是拉肚子，肚子咕噜噜叫，这几天爱放屁，刚刚肚子疼 Patient:I always have diarrhea and my stomach is purring.I love farting these days. I just have stomachache. 医生：您好，请问出现这种情况有多长时间了呢？您的饮食和生活规律吗。 Doctor:Hello, how long has this happened? Do you have a diet and lifestyle. 患者：饮食规律，就因为精神萎靡，没吃饭，并且没有饥饿感。 Patient:Eating regularly, because of mental depression, no food, and no sense of hunger. 医生：像您的这种情况还是考虑肠道的问题，至于有没有炎症？还需要做一个大便常规的检测来看一下。 Doctor:In your case,I still consider the intestinal tract. As for whether there is inflammation? We also need to do a routine stool test. 患者：排气从前天晚上就开始，无味，但昨天和今天中午大便还有点干燥。 Patient: the exhaust started the night before yesterday. It's tasteless, but the stool was still a little dry yesterday and at noon today.	**RNN** 嗯嗯，这个症状多长时间了，嗯嗯，谢谢啦，没事。 Uh huh, how long has this symptom been? Uh huh, thank you. It's okay. **GPT-2** 您的情况建议做一个胃镜，目前考虑是胃炎，如果感觉情况严重，可以服用一些整肠生，有一定的缓解作用。 It is suggested to have a gastroscope for your situation. At present, gastritis is considered. If you feel the situation is serious, you can take some bowel rectification, which has a certain alleviating effect. **MT5-base** 如果有腹泻，可以吃点金双歧，如果没有症状，可以吃点益生菌，比如培菲康。 If you have diarrhea, you can eat Golden bifid.If you have no symptoms,you can eat probiotics, such as peifeikang. **T5-medicine** 您的情况还是考虑肠道功能紊乱，建议您可以吃点益生菌，如整肠生，益生元等。还可以服用整肠生和金双歧调理一下。 Your situation still considers intestinal dysfunction.It is suggested that you can eat probiotics,such as whole bowel,prebiotics, etc.You can also take whole intestines and Golden Bifid for conditioning.

Note: The left part of the table is the basic dialogue between doctors and patients, and the right part is the final reply made by different models based on this.

Comparing the segmentation based on "word" granularity with based on "words and expressions" in T5-medicine, it is verified that the segmentation based on "words and expressions" granularity is better than based on "word" granularity in Chinese dialogue task, and BLEU-AVE increases significantly. Because the division based on "words and expressions" granularity reduces the uncertainty of word meaning, reduces the complexity of model and can well alleviate the problem of exposure bias. The evaluation results are shown in Table 5:

Table 5. The "word" segmentation based on word granularity and "words and expressions"

Segmentation	Entity-F1	BLEU-AVE
Words and expressions	**0.2644**	**0.1268**
word	0.2423	0.0978

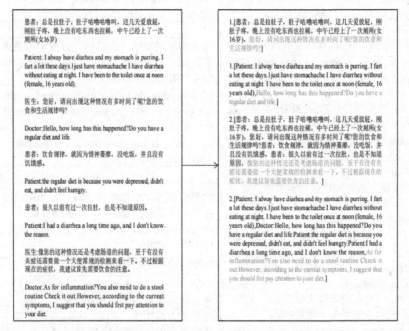

Fig. 2. In the chart, the left part is the original data and the right part is the result of pretreatment. The black font is the constructed "dialogue" and the red font is the doctor's reply "result".

5 Summary

In this ccks2021 (China Conference on Knowledge Graph and Semantic Computing) of entity generation task containing Chinese, and T5-medicine is adopted. Firstly, medical corpus is used to pre-training the initial model to make the model have a deeper understanding of medical content. This end-to-end approach, from input to model and then output, ignores the internal details, thus simplifying the process of task processing. Even when there is less label data on our hand, this pre-trained model can still play a good effect. The feasibility of this pre-trained model with large parameters in Chinese text generation is verified. The effect of word segmentation based on "words and expressions" is better than that based on "word". For the combination of most common words, the model will have a deeper understanding of professional words, and will also have a gratifying effect in the process of predicting recall.

Acknowledgments. This work was supported by the National Natural Science Foundation of China (Grant No. 61976156, No. 11803022 and No. 61702367), Tianjin Science and Technology Commissioner project (No. 20YDTPJC00560), the Natural Science Foundation of Tianjin (Grant No. 19JCYBJC15300), and the Research Project of Tianjin Municipal Commission of Education (No. 2018KJ105 and No. 2018KJ106).

References

1. Liu, W., Tang, J., Qin, J., Xu, L., Li, Z., Liang, X.: MedDG: a large-scale medical consultation dataset for building medical dialogue system. arXiv preprint arXiv:2010.07497 (2020)
2. Li, X., Chen, Y.-N., Li, L., Gao, J.: End-to-end task-completion neural dialogue systems. arXiv preprint arXiv:1703.01008 (2018)
3. Huang, Z., Xu, W., Yu, K.: Bidirectional LSTM-CRF models for sequence tagging. arXiv preprint arXiv:1508.01991 (2015)
4. Na, D., Hao, F., Xu, C.: Named entity recognition of traditional chinese medicine patents based on BiLSTM-CRF. Wirel. Commun. Mob. Comput. **2021**(2), 1–12 (2021)
5. Zeng, G., Yang, W., Ju, Z., Yang, Y.: Meddialog: a large-scale medical dialogue dataset. In: Proceedings of the 2020 Conference on Empirical Methods in Natural Language Processing, pp. 9241–9250 (2020)
6. Xu, L., Zhou, Q., Gong, K., Liang, X., Tang, J., Lin, L.: End-to-end knowledge routed relational dialogue system for automatic diagnosis. arXiv preprint arXiv:1901.10623 (2019)
7. Shivade, C., Raghavan, P., Fosler-Lussier, E., Embi, P.J.: A review of approaches to identifying patient phenotype cohorts using electronic health records. J. Am. Med. Inf. Assoc. **21**(2), 221–230 (2014)
8. Liu, Q., Wei, Z., Peng, B., Dai, X.: Task-oriented dialogue system for automatic diagnosis. In: Proceedings of the 56th Annual Meeting of the Association for Computational Linguistics, pp. 201–207 (2018)
9. Liao, K., Liu, Q., Wei, Z., Peng, B., Chen, Q.: Task-oriented dialogue system for automatic disease diagnosis via hierarchical reinforcement learning. arXiv preprint: arXiv:2004.14254 (2020)
10. Budzianowski, P., Vulic, I.: Hello, it's gpt-2-how can i help you? towards the use of pre-trained language models for task-oriented dialogue systems. arXiv preprint: arXiv:1907.05774 (2019)
11. Papineni, K., Roukos, S., Ward, T.: BLEU: a method for automatic evaluation of machine translation. In: Proceedings of the 40th Annual Meeting of the Association for Computational Linguistics, pp. 311–318 (2002)
12. Liu, Z., Wang, H., Niu, Z.-Y., Wu, H., Che, W., Liu, T.: Towards conversational recommendation over multi-type dialogs. arXiv preprint: arXiv:2005.03954 (2020)

Enhance Both Text and Label: Combination Strategies for Improving the Generalization Ability of Medical Entity Extraction

Zhen Gan[1,3], Zhucong Li[1,2], Baoli Zhang[1], Jing Wan[3], Yubo Chen[1,2(✉)], Kang Liu[1,2], Jun Zhao[1,2(✉)], Yafei Shi[4], and Shengping Liu[4]

[1] National Laboratory of Pattern Recognition, Institute of Automation, Chinese Academy of Sciences, Beijing, China
{zhucong.li,baoli.zhang,yubo.chen,kliu,jzhao}@nlpr.ia.ac.cn
[2] School of Artificial Intelligence, University of Chinese Academy of Sciences, Beijing, China
[3] Beijing University of Chemical Technology, Beijing, China
{ganzhen,wanj}@mail.buct.edu.cn
[4] Beijing Unisound Information Technology Co., Ltd., Beijing, China
{shiyafei,liushengping}@unisound.com

Abstract. This paper describes our approach for the Chinese medical Named Entity Recognition (NER) and event extraction tasks organized by the China Conference on Knowledge Graph and Semantic Computing (CCKS) 2021. For the NER task, we need to identify the entity boundaries and category labels of six types of entities from Chinese electronic medical records (EMR). And for the Event Extraction task, we need to recognizes a type of tumor event from Chinese EMR, which contains three tumor-related attributes. This medical entity and event extraction task has two main challenges: 1) How to build a unified modeling framework for entity and event extraction. 2) How to improve the generalization ability of medical entity extraction. For these two challenges, we use a sequence labeling framework based on entity extraction to unify the above two tasks. Based on the pre-trained model, we propose a combined strategy of unsupervised text mode enhancement and label mode enhancement. In the end, it ranked second without any post-processing.

Keywords: Named Entity Recognition · Event extraction · Electronic medical records

1 Introduction

1.1 Task Definition

The first task is Chinese medical NER, that is, for a given set of Chinese electronic medical records (EMRs) plain text documents, identify and extract the

B. Qin et al. (Eds.): CCKS 2021, CCIS 1553, pp. 92–101, 2022.
https://doi.org/10.1007/978-981-19-0713-5_11

entity mentions related to medical clinical practice, and classify them into pre-defined six categories, including disease, imaging examination, laboratory examination, drug, operation, and anatomy. The second task is Event Extraction from Chinese medical records. Given the electronic medical record text data, its main entity is tumor, which defines several attributes of tumor events, including tumor size, tumor primary site, and metastasis site. We need to identify and extract events and attributes to construct text.

1.2   Overview of Main Challenges and Solutions

For this mission, we have two main challenges This paper introduces uncertainty as an algorithm modeling strategy towards the two significant challenges in this competition.

The first challenge is how to build a unified modeling framework for entity and event extraction. Entity extraction aims to identify the boundaries and categories of entities in medical texts, while event extraction aims to extract specified event attributes from medical texts. This event extraction task only involves the extraction of three attribute entities corresponding to the main tumor entity, and there is a clear sequence relationship between attribute entities, so we use a sequence annotation framework based on entity extraction to unify the above two tasks.

The second challenge is how to improve the generalization ability of medical entity extraction. The generalization ability of a model usually depends largely on the richness of text features and label features in the training data. In order to make full use of the limited labeled data and unlabeled data in the dataset, we propose a combination strategy of unsupervised text mode enhancement and label mode enhancement based on the pre-training model. In the end, without any post-processing, it ranked second overall.

2   Our Method

2.1   Basic Model Structure

We use a framework based on sequence labeling to uniformly solve NER and event extraction tasks. The basic model structure of our framework based on sequence labeling is shown in Fig. 1. The input samples get their embedding representation through the pre-training model [2]. Then the input after the embedding representation is connected to Bi-directional Long Short-Term Memory (BiLSTM) [4,7,13] for context encoding, and finally Conditional Random Field (CRF) [3,11] is used to decode the output of the BiLSTM layer.

2.2   Unsupervised Text Mode Enhancement Strategy

The lack of electronic medical record data makes the model see fewer text patterns, which greatly affects the generalization of the model.

The place where the data attribute entity of the event appears is uncertain. For example, the description of "transfer location" can appear at any position at the beginning, end, and middle of the sample. In this way, the position of the "metastasis" appears more random. We hope that every text model has more samples. In addition, the description of tumor events is complex and diverse. The size and metastasis of each tumor are complex and diverse. Most of these descriptions are within one sentence, so we hope that each tumor's primary site has more tumor sizes. Description and description of the metastasis site.

Based on the above analysis, we have adopted three main text mode enhancement strategies:

- The order of sample sentences is randomly shuffled;
- The order of the sample sentences is reversed;
- The order of sentences among the data set samples is randomly combined.

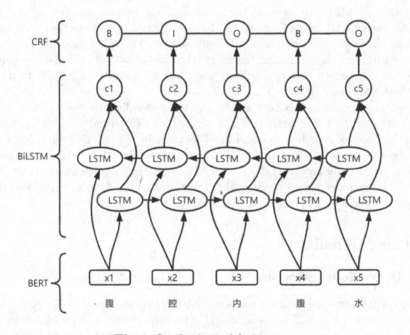

Fig. 1. Our basic model structure.

Pre-training Model Continues Pre-training. In order to make the language model more adaptable to the fields of cancer and imaging, we crawled a large number of data texts in the medical field from "Baidu Baike" and "Quick Ask Doctor Net". After the above text mode enhancement strategy, we obtained 200,000 medical texts. We perform 10-round mask language model pre-training on medical text.

In order to further adapt the language model to the specific text mode of the NER task and the Event Extraction task, we respectively enhance the text of the training data of the two tasks:

NER: Using all text data, a total of 2500 medical records (including labeled data and unlabeled data). The data is processed into text fragments less than 510 length, a total of 3602 pieces of data.

Event Extraction: All text data, a total of 3000 medical records (including labeled data and unlabeled data), and data enhancement, the enhanced data is processed into text fragments less than 510 length, a total of 10550 data.

Finally, we perform 100 rounds of mask language model pre-training on the enhanced training text. The above process does not use training data labels. Such an unsupervised enhancement strategy allows the pre-training model to learn more and more relevant text patterns.

2.3   Semi-supervised Label Mode Enhancement Strategy

There is less data to annotate electronic medical records, some types of labels are few, and lack of diversity. Our model cannot learn such a long-tail label model.

The organizer provided additional unlabeled data. This part of the electronic medical record is for us to look for more diversified label data. How to use the label pattern contained in this part of the data is an important issue.

The semi-supervised label mode enhancement strategy is mainly divided into two steps:

- Use labeled data for training and label unlabeled data;
- Add the obtained pseudo-label data to the training set, and train to obtain the final model.

2.4   Model Training

Five-Fold Cross-Voting. We use the idea of five-fold cross-validation to divide the training set into five different data sets. Each data set has a different validation set, and the distribution of their entity labels is different. We use the same model to train five models on the five datasets, then use the five models to predict on the test dataset, and perform hard voting on the prediction results to obtain the fusion result of the five models.

Model Ensemble. To further reduce the impact of the randomness of the model parameters on the prediction results, we ensemble a variety of models through voting to weaken the impact of performance fluctuations caused by a single model parameter change on the prediction results.

Figure 2 shows the process of model ensemble combined with five-fold cross-voting [5]. There are three voting methods. The first voting method is shown in the black box. The black box indicates that the 5 models trained in the same training set are first fused, and then the 5 fusion models obtained from the 5 data sets continue to be fused, for a total of 25 models. The second voting method is shown in the orange box. In the orange box, first retrieve the 5 models retrieved from the 5-fold data set of each model structure, and then the 5 models retrieved from the 5 model results are merged into a total of 25 models. The results of the two voting methods are similar. For the third voting method, We can also use 25 models for direct voting fusion.

In our experiment, for NER and event extraction tasks, we used two model frameworks and trained five models with five-fold data sets, a total of 10 models. And the final ten prediction results were voted and fused.

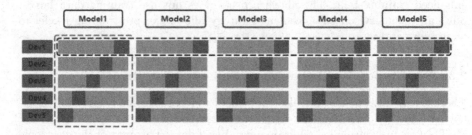

Fig. 2. The process of model ensemble.

Adversarial Training. With reference to the FGM [9] adversarial training mechanism [8,12], we added a small disturbance to the embedding layer of the model. The input text sequence of the model is $[v_1, v_2, \ldots, v_T]$, and its embedding is expressed as x. Then the small disturbance r_{adv} applied each time is:

$$r_{adv} = \epsilon \cdot g/\|g\|_2 \qquad (1)$$

$$g = \nabla_x L(\theta, x, y) \qquad (2)$$

The meaning of the formula is to move the input along the direction of the gradient, so that the model loss rises at the fastest speed, thereby forming an attack. In order to fight against such an attack, the model needs to learn such adversarial examples and look for more robust parameters in the optimization process.

3 Experiments

3.1 Dataset

There are two medical electronic medical records datasets, one is the NER dataset and the other is the event dataset. Data information is shown in Table 1.

The CCKS 2021 Medical Named Entity Recognition Competition provides 1,500 labeled data as a training set. The data includes labels for six types of entities, including disease & diagnosis, imaging examination, laboratory examination, operation, drug, and anatomy. Besides, the task also provided 1,000 unlabeled data. The final test data has only 100 medical records.

The CCKS 2021 Medical Event Extraction Competition provides 1,400 labeled data as a training set. The main entity of this data is tumor, which defines several attributes of tumor events, such as tumor size, tumor primary site, and metastasis site. And the task provided 1,300 unlabeled data. The final test data has 300 medical records.

Table 1. The statistics of the number of sentences in the two datasets

Dataset	Train	Test	Unlabeled data
NER	1500	100	1000
Event extraction	1400	300	1300

3.2   Evaluation

For the fairness of model comparison, we refer to the standard-setting and use the micro-average F1 score to evaluate all methods, and report the precision and recall as percentages.

3.3   Pre-processing

For the NER task, we mainly adopted the data preprocessing of text normalization and long text segmentation. For the Event task, we also performed the preprocessing of the answer position return mark. The detailed description is as follows.

- **Text Normalization.** This step aims to deal with illegal characters and redundant text information in the original data and normalize it. Specific cleaning strategies include: converting full-width numbers and letters into half-width, and English letters uniformly converted to lowercase; using uniform symbols to replace special characters, such as invisible characters, spaces, etc.; reducing repeated non-text symbols to one symbol, such as repetition After the five spaces are processed, there is only one space.
- **Sentence Segmentation.** Since the maximum input sequence of the data BERT model is only 510, the input long text is segmented under the premise of ensuring the relatively complete semantic information in the office to ensure that the text length of each input BERT is less than 510.
- **Answer Annotation.** For event extraction tasks, the training data provided by the organizer only has answers corresponding to the target slot. We use the sequence labeling model to model the slot filling task, and we need to label the position of the answer in the input text.

3.4   Implementation Details

Implementation details of our two models are shown in Table 2.

Medical_bert_wwm+BiLSTM+CRF. This model uses the Chinese version of the medical pre-training model released by PCL PENG CHENG LABORA- TORY, named PCL-MedBERT-wwm.[1] In the implementation, take the last layer of PCL-MedBERT-wwm, a total of 768 is used as the input of BiLSTM, and the hidden layer unit of BiLSTM takes 768. Finally, a fully connected layer of 768*2 hidden units is connected to the CRF to calculate the final output tag. The batch size is 8, the learning rate of the PCL-MedBERT-wwm part is 5e-5, the learning rate of the BiLSTM+CRF part is 5e-3, the training is 50 epoch, and AdamW [6] is used as the optimizer. The model uses dropout [10] and is set to 0.3.

RoBERTa_wwm_ext_large [1] **+BiLSTM+CRF.** This model uses the RoBERTa_wwm_ext_large model released by Harbin Institute of Technology. In the implementation, the last layer of RoBERTa_wwm_ext_large is taken, 1024 is used as the input of BiLSTM, and the hidden layer unit of BiLSTM is 1024. Finally, a fully connected layer of 1024*2 hidden units is connected to the CRF to calculate the final output tag. The batch size is 2, the learning rate of the RoBERTa_wwm_ext_large part is 3e-5, the learning rate of the BiLSTM + CRF part is 5e-4, the training is 20 epoch, and AdamW is used as the optimizer. The model uses dropout and is set to 0.3.

Table 2. The details of our experimental parameter. Note: the Medical means Medical_bert_wwm+BiLSTM+CRF, and the RoBERTa means RoBERTa_wwm_ext_la- rge+BiLSTM+CRF.

Model	Learning rate	Epoch	Dropout	Optimizer
Medical	5e-5	50	0.3	AdamW
RoBERTa	3e-5	20	0.3	AdamW

3.5   Results

We conducted a large number of experiments on two subtasks. We divided the training data into five-fold data sets and conducted experiments separately. The main results for the NER task are shown in Table 3. The main results of the Event task are shown in Table 4.

---

[1] https://code.ihub.org.cn/projects/1775/files.

Table 3. The main results of local experiments on NER task.

Model	data0	data1	data2	data3	data4
BERT_base	83.53	84.40	83.88	84.42	85.00
Medical	84.27	85.38	84.71	85.81	85.70
Medical+PT	84.58	85.97	84.88	85.97	86.11
Medical+FGM	84.83	86.01	84.91	86.11	86.24
Medical+PT+FGM	84.73	86.25	85.32	86.43	86.09
Medical+FGM+SLE	**85.82**	86.73	86.62	87.93	87.17
Medical+PT+FGM+SLE	**85.70**	**86.89**	**86.74**	**87.77**	**87.51**
RoBERTa	83.78	84.71	84.11	85.49	84.91
RoBERTa+FGM+SLE	**85.72**	**86.55**	**86.63**	**87.53**	**87.01**

The data0-4 represent five-fold data sets respectively. The BERT_base represents the abbreviation of BERT_base [2] +BiLSTM+CRF. The Medical represents the abbreviation of Medical_bert_wwm+BiLSTM+CRF, and The RoBERTa represents the abbreviation of RoBERTa_wwm_ext_large+BiLSTM+CRF. The FGM represents our adversarial Training, PT means to continue pre-training, and the SLE means semi-supervised label mode enhancement strategy. The scores are F1-score as percentages.

Table 4. The main results of local experiments on Event Extraction task.

Model	data0	data1	data2	data3	data4
BERT_base	75.27	67.75	60.77	76.13	80.19
Medical	77.47	69.91	62.95	75.97	81.75
Medical+PT	**79.32**	72.35	62.64	**77.58**	**82.47**
Medical+FGM	77.23	70.26	62.56	77.73	82.30
Medical+PT+FGM	**79.03**	**74.34**	**65.13**	**77.50**	**82.42**
RoBERTa	75.47	68.70	57.45	74.61	80.32
RoBERTa+FGM	76.96	70.42	62.00	76.62	80.83

For the NER task, our model is significantly improved compared to the basic BERT_base model, which is about 2 to 3% points higher. Whether in Medical_bert_wwm or RoBERTa_wwm_ext, our method can improve the improvement of about 2% compared with the basic model. The PT has an average improvement of 0.5% for the model. The FGM can bring about 0.6% improvement. SLE also has good improvement effect.

For Event Extraction tasks, our model is also significantly improved compared to the basic BERT_base model, with an average increase of 3.66%. In the data0 data, Medical+PT has increased by 4.05% compared with BERT_base, and has increased by 1.85% compared with the basic Medical_bert_wwm. Compared with Medical_bert_wwm, the experimental results on RoBERTa_wwm_ext are not ideal, which shows that after pre-training on medical data, the performance of the pre-training model can be effectively improved.

4   Conclusions

In order to solve the challenges brought by these two tasks, we use a sequence labeling framework based on entity extraction to unify the above two tasks, and propose a combination strategy of unsupervised text mode enhancement and label mode enhancement to continue pre-training, so as to achieve Good performance.

How to better perform joint extraction between Chinese medical Named entity recognition and event extraction tasks is our future research goal.

Acknowledgement. This work is supported by the National Key Research and Development Program of China (No. 2020AAA0106400). This work is supported by the National Natural Science Foundation of China (No. 61922085, No. 61806201). This work is also supported by the CCF-Tencent Open Research Fund, the Beijing Academy of Artificial Intelligence (BAAI2019QN0301), the Key Research Program of the Chinese Academy of Sciences (Grant No. ZDBS-SSW-JSC006) and the Youth Innovation Promotion Association CAS.

References

1. Cui, Y., Che, W., Liu, T., Qin, B., Wang, S., Hu, G.: Revisiting pre-trained models for Chinese natural language processing. In: Findings of EMNLP. Association for Computational Linguistics (2020)
2. Devlin, J., Chang, M.W., Lee, K., Toutanova, K.: Bert: pre-training of deep bidirectional transformers for language understanding. In: Proceedings of the 2019 Conference of the North American Chapter of the Association for Computational Linguistics: Human Language Technologies, Volume 1 (Long and Short Papers), pp. 4171–4186 (2019)
3. Lafferty, J.D., McCallum, A., Pereira, F.C.: Conditional random fields: probabilistic models for segmenting and labeling sequence data. In: Proceedings of the Eighteenth International Conference on Machine Learning, pp. 282–289 (2001)
4. Lample, G., Ballesteros, M., Subramanian, S., Kawakami, K., Dyer, C.: Neural architectures for named entity recognition. In: Proceedings of the 2016 Conference of the North American Chapter of the Association for Computational Linguistics: Human Language Technologies, pp. 260–270 (2016)
5. Li, Z., et al.: Semi-supervised noisy label learning for Chinese medical named entity recognition. Data Intell. **3**, 1–10 (2021)
6. Loshchilov, I., Hutter, F.: Fixing weight decay regularization in adam (2018)
7. Ma, X., Hovy, E.: End-to-end sequence labeling via bi-directional LSTM-CNNs-CRF. In: Proceedings of the 54th Annual Meeting of the Association for Computational Linguistics (Volume 1: Long Papers), pp. 1064–1074 (2016)

8. Madry, A., Makelov, A., Schmidt, L., Tsipras, D., Vladu, A.: Towards deep learning models resistant to adversarial attacks. arXiv preprint arXiv:1706.06083 (2017)
9. Miyato, T., Dai, A.M., Goodfellow, I.: Adversarial training methods for semi-supervised text classification. arXiv preprint arXiv:1605.07725 (2016)
10. Srivastava, N., Hinton, G., Krizhevsky, A., Sutskever, I., Salakhutdinov, R.: Dropout: a simple way to prevent neural networks from overfitting. J. Mach. Learn. Res. **15**(1), 1929–1958 (2014)
11. Sutton, C., McCallum, A.: An introduction to conditional random fields for relational learning. Introd. Stat. Relat. Learn. **2**, 93–128 (2006)
12. Szegedy, C., et al.: Intriguing properties of neural networks. arXiv preprint arXiv:1312.6199 (2013)
13. Xu, K., Zhou, Z., Hao, T., Liu, W.: A bidirectional LSTM and conditional random fields approach to medical named entity recognition. In: Hassanien, A.E., Shaalan, K., Gaber, T., Tolba, M.F. (eds.) AISI 2017. AISC, vol. 639, pp. 355–365. Springer, Cham (2018). https://doi.org/10.1007/978-3-319-64861-3_33

Knowledge-Enhanced Retrieval:
A Scheme for Question Answering

Fake Lin[1], Weican Cao[2], Wen Zhang[2], Liyi Chen[1], Yuan Hong[2], Tong Xu[1(✉)],
and Chang Tan[2]

[1] University of Science and Technology of China, Hefei, China
fklin@mail.ustc.edu.cn, liyichencly@gmail.com, tongxu@ustc.edu.cn
[2] iFLYTEK Co., Ltd., Hefei, China
{wccao,wenzhang9,yuanhong2,changtan2}@iflytek.com

Abstract. Chinese Knowledge Base Question Answering (CKBQA), as
a significant task in natural language processing, has drawn massive
attention from both industry and academia. However, previous studies
mainly concentrated on multi-hop questions, which may limit the performance of tackling complex natural questions with various forms. To
that end, in this paper, we propose a comprehensive technical framework
called Knowledge-Enhanced Retrieval Question Answering (KERQA)
for tackling complex questions, which could precisely extract the gold
answers to these questions from a large-scale knowledge graph. Specifically, our proposed KERQA follows the pipeline with five modules,
including the *Question Classification* module to categorize questions, the
Named Entity Recognition module to extract mentions, and the *Entity
Linking* module to match entities in the knowledge graph (KG). Along
this line, we further design the *Path Generation* module to associate the
paths in the KG with predefined templates, as well as the *Path Ranking*
module to capture the best path. Extensive validations demonstrate the
effectiveness of our KERQA framework, which achieved an F1 score of
78.78% on the final leaderboard of the CCKS 2021 KBQA contest.

Keywords: Knowledge base question answering · Machine reading
comprehension · Contrastive learning

1 Introduction

Recent years have witnessed the booming of Chinese knowledge base question
answering (CKBQA), which could automatically answer the questions in Chinese
language based on the structured information in Knowledge Graph (KG). Along
this line, CKBQA has become prevalent in broad domains due to its powerful
interpretability and reasoning capabilities.

Traditionally, large efforts have been made on KBQA tasks, which could
be roughly divided into two categories, i.e., *semantic parsing* and *information
retrieval* solutions. On the one hand, semantic parsing (SP) [9,10] solutions

ⓒ Springer Nature Singapore Pte Ltd. 2022
B. Qin et al. (Eds.): CCKS 2021, CCIS 1553, pp. 102–113, 2022.
https://doi.org/10.1007/978-981-19-0713-5_12

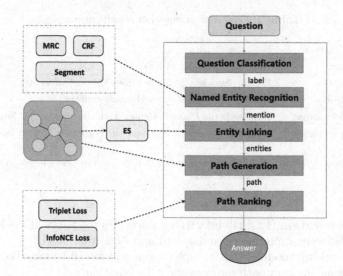

Fig. 1. Architecture of KERQA.

mainly transform natural language questions into a logical form with rich information, and then capture the answers via the logical form aligning to the knowledge graph. On the other hand, information retrieval (IR) [7,8] solutions mainly retrieve paths in KG through searching entities staged in the question, and then rank them to obtain the final answer.

However, most existing approaches manifest the limitation in dealing with more complicated questions. For example, current solutions may fail to answer the question "What are the attractions around the Forbidden City in Beijing within 5 km", since they may treat the "5 km" as a specific entity, rather than a distance feature. In this case, they could not approximate the digital values to match correct entities within certain distance, e.g., "4.99 km". Even worse, considering that these features are usually denoted as Compound Value Type (CVT) nodes in KG, when retrieving the answers, these CVT nodes next to "the Forbidden City" entity could be probably treated as answers, but not the correct answers like POIs. This phenomenon may further increase the difficulty of KG reasoning for KBQA.

To that end, in this paper, we propose a novel Knowledge-Enhanced Retrieval Question Answering (KERQA) framework to precisely extract the gold answers to these questions from a large-scale knowledge graph. Specifically, the architecture of KERQA is shown in Fig. 1, which consists of five modules, including:

- **Question Classification** (QC) module, which categorizes the question into six categories.
- **Named Entity Recognition** (NER) module, which extracts mentions (i.e. keywords) from the question content.
- **Entity Linking** (EL) module, which matches extracted mentions with corresponding entities in knowledge graph.

Table 1. Overview of question classification.

Label	Description	Example
label-1	1-hop	Who is the founder of KFC?
label-2	Squeeze	Which physicists graduated from Peking University?
label-3	Multi-hop	What is the capital of Beethoven's country?
label-4	Two locations	How far is the Phoenix Center from the Shenyu Art Museum?
label-5	Neighborhood	What are the attractions near the Forbidden City in Beijing within 5 km
label-6	Squeeze & 1-hop	How much is the reward for the man in One Piece who invented the weather rod

- **Path Generation** (PG) module, which associates the paths in the KG with our predefined templates selected according to question label.
- **Path Ranking** module, which employs a neural model to rank these paths for choosing the best path for answering the question.

Finally, extensive validations with ablation studies have demonstrated the effectiveness of our KERQA framework, which achieved an F1 score of 78.78% on the final leaderboard of CCKS 2021 KBQA contest.

2   Methodology

2.1   Question Classification

Question classification is the first module in our KERQA framework, which targets at tackling different problems in terms of the question label. This module will stop in early stage if the number of mentions is not enough to fill the slots in NER module. Moreover, it will select the corresponding template to construct a more accurate path in PG module. As shown in Table 1, we classify all questions into six categories, namely 1-hop, squeeze, multi-hop, two locations, neighborhood, squeeze & 1-hop.

In detail, we leverage the pre-trained BERT model, which has achieved state-of-the-art performance on downstream NLP tasks. Moreover, we add a fully connected layer and a softmax layer in BERT for our classification task to output the probability of each classification, and then select the classification label with highest probability as the result.

2.2   Named Entity Recognition

NER module, as the second module, allows us to extract mentions from a question, which is the most critical component in the entire pipeline. If we fail to recall the mentions, the framework will suffer from propagation error, i.e. the mistakes of NER would affect the following tasks. Therefore, in order to assure the recall rate of mentions, this module integrates four parts, i.e., BERT+CRF, Machine Reading Comprehension (MRC), Rules and LAC.

BERT+CRF. BERT+CRF specializes in dealing with NER task due to its versatility, simplicity and effectiveness. In practice, we continue to use BERT followed by CRF layer, which regulates the format of the output to make the result more compatible with the NER task. However, the model does not achieve the desired effect owing to NER annotation failures and errors. More annotation details can be found in Sect. 3.1.

Machine Reading Comprehension. We apply MRC [1] as another model for NER module, which is widely used in NER task. According to [1], we can treat the MRC task as a NER task, with the adaption that the "query" will be set as the "mentions in the question". What should be noted is that MRC can solve the overlapping problem of mentions, i.e. a single token is assigned to multiple mentions. For instance, for question "what are the hotels near Nanjing Metropark Hotel", "Nanjing" is mentioned twice, both in "Nanjing Metropark Hotel" and "Nanjing", while classical approaches in NER task such as BERT+CRF could just recognize one of them.

Rules. We utilize some rules for matching special formats, such as dates, book titles or double-quotes. Specifically, Regular Expression is a common and efficient way to match these patterns and retrieve the related spans, and then we add these spans to the mention list. In particular, considering that there are various date forms in dataset, we have unified them as "yyyy-MM-dd", e.g. "June 1, 2004" would be transformed into "2004-06-01".

LAC. A word segmentation system LAC is used to avoid missing the mentions that have not appeared in training set, because LAC has been trained by numerous corpora and thus has better generalization. At the same time, we filter some frequently used nouns, e.g., "works", "city" and "songs", to reduce the number of irrelevant mentions.

2.3 Entity Linking

Because of millions of entities in KG, it is hard to directly recognize the gold entity when given a mention. In this paper, CKRQA employs *Entity Linking* (*Entity Disambiguation*) to select the top-k candidate entities based on the text matching and the popularity of the entities (i.e. the degrees of the entity). Here we deploy the ElasticSearch (ES) tool, but not apply a model, since the introduction of text matching and popularity already has promising performance on this job. Along this line, we construct the candidate entity list via the following information:

- For entities that have a perfect text match to the mention, we can directly add these entities to the list.

Table 2. Path templates.

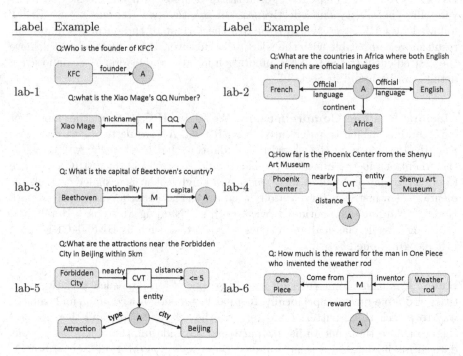

Label	Example	Label	Example
lab-1	Q:Who is the founder of KFC? / Q:what is the Xiao Mage's QQ Number?	lab-2	Q:What are the countries in Africa where both English and French are official languages
lab-3	Q: What is the capital of Beethoven's country?	lab-4	Q:How far is the Phoenix Center from the Shenyu Art Museum
lab-5	Q:What are the attractions near the Forbidden City in Beijing within 5km	lab-6	Q: How much is the reward for the man in One Piece who invented the weather rod

- For entities that have a partial match to the mention, we employ ES for fuzzy matching to pick the entities with the top m score. Moreover, we also take the popularity of the entity into account, because an entity including more edges is more likely to be chosen.
- For entities that completely mismatch with the mention, such as "Ironman" mapping to the entity "⟨Stark⟩", we retrieve the entities from the dictionary offered by competition organizers to deal with this kind of issue.

Finally, we collect about 5 candidate entities for each mention, and then feed these mention-entity pairs into the next module.

2.4   Path Generation

Following the entities obtained in Sect. 2.3, *Path Generation* module targets at producing candidate paths over KG. To this end, we have defined a set of path templates, which are also divided into six categories as in Sect. 2.1. We will then fill the slots in the templates with entities to get candidate paths. We illustrate examples of each category in Table 2.

Traditional works [5,6] usually regarded a template as a structure with a specific number of slots. A structure with 2 slots and one with 3 slots will be perceived as two different templates. Thus failing to estimate the number of

Table 3. Path templates to generate sentences.

Question and Correct Path	Sentences
Q: What is the capital of Beethoven's country? Beethoven →nationality→ M →capital→ A	A1:the capital of the nationality of Beethoven A2:the name of the nationality of Beethoven A3:the nationality of the nephew of Beethoven
Q:What are the countries in Africa where both English and French are official languages French →Official language→ A →Official language→ English A →continent→ Africa	A1:Both English and French are official language and Africa is continent A2:Both English and French are language and Africa is area A3:English is official language and Africa is country

entities will prevent us from finding the right template. To decrease the impact of misestimation, we turn to the overall structure of the question to define the template instead of the number of slots in the template. Then we will present the process of how to fill the slots in the template.

- (1) We first use the candidate mentions to create sequences with n mentions in a combinatorial manner, where n is the number of mentions per sequence in current round. Initially, n is assigned as $min(m, b)$, m denotes the number of candidate mentions and b represents the hyper-parameter to prevent the number of sequences from exploding.
- (2) Next we iterate sequences generated in step (1). Given a mention sequence, we use the entities from each corresponding mention-entity pair to replace the mentions in the sequence. Note that a mention-entity pair has approximately 5 candidate entities, we will produce nearly 625 entity sequences in a 3-mention sequence. These entity sequences will be put into the template as the slots in turn to match the path in KG.
- (3) Finally, we have three branches according to the matching result: (a) If we successfully find at least one path, then we add these paths to the path list and then exit this process. (b) If we fail to find a path and n is greater than 1, we will set n as $n - 1$ and return to step (1). (c) If n is equal to 1, this program is considered a match failure and exits.

This approach removes the requirement to identify the number of slots and manages to cope with the 4-entity cases without any modification.

At the same time, the challenge staged in Sect. 1 can be easily solved via neighborhood template. For the question mentioned in Table 2 (neighborhood), we first recognize the entities "attractions", "the Forbidden City", "Beijing" and "5 km" from the previous modules. Then as we get the result of classification "label-5", the distance information such as "5 km" will be converted to an approximately digital match node and filled into the slot that is connected to the CVT node. Next we look up the surrounding nodes of entities and find that

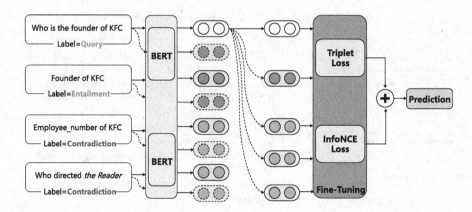

Fig. 2. Architecture of the path ranking.

only "the Forbidden City" has CVT nodes around it. Therefore "the Forbidden City" serves as the starting point and it is placed in the appropriate slot as well. Eventually the remaining entities (i.e. "attractions" and "Beijing") will perform operations similar to label-2 to expand the template.

2.5 Path Ranking

Given the candidate paths, finally, the *Path Ranking* module is designed to select a gold path as our final answer. Before sorting paths, we need to figure out how to make structured information (i.e. paths) comparable with unstructured information (i.e. natural language). To tackle this issue, we define sentence generation rules for every template to transform the candidate paths into natural language. Examples are shown in Table 3. The sentences in red are the gold sentences, and their relevant paths are on the left, while the paths of wrong sentences do not appear in this table. In this way, we can now consider this task as a classical NLP similarity task.

We will introduce the motivation and the models of *Path Ranking* module in the following. Note that BERT is also our basic model for its extraordinary performance. Nevertheless, the word embeddings learned by BERT show a long-tail distribution owing to the imbalance of word frequencies. In other words, embeddings of high-frequency words are more clustered and close to the origin, whereas the embeddings of low-frequency words are more scattered and far from the origin, leading to the overall sentence embedding being more sensitive to the changes in high-frequency words while ignoring low-frequency words that may actually have more semantic information. In light of [3], we present a supervised contrastive learning model to calculate an appropriate semantic matching score for each candidate path. The architecture of the model is shown in Fig. 2.

To be more specific, we first convert the raw data processed in Sect. 3.1 to a set of training data (x, x^+, x^-), where x is the original question, x^+ is the positive sentence (entailment) which is generated by gold path and x^- is the negative sentence (contradiction) generated by the wrong path. Before feeding these data into the model, we perform a data augment via dropout, which is a supplement to the insufficient data. Inspired by [2,3], we then employ Online Triplet Mining Strategy to dynamically compute the hard and semi-hard data as the model output. The motivation of this training procedure is to make the embeddings of x and x^+ close while keeping the embeddings of x and x^- far away from each other. To this end, we adopt two objectives: Triplet Loss and InfoNCE Loss [3]. The definition of the Triplet Loss is:

$$\mathcal{L}\left(h, h^+, h^-\right) = \max\left(0, d\left(h, h^+\right)^2 - d\left(h, h^-\right)^2 + m\right), \tag{1}$$

where h represents the pool vector of sentences, $d(:,:)$ is a method for calculating distance between two embeddings, such as Euclidean distance, and m controls the margin between $d\left(h, h^+\right)$ and $d\left(h, h^-\right)$. Basically, if the distance between $\left(h, h^+\right)^2$ and $d\left(h, h^-\right)^2$ is greater than the margin, the loss function no longer penalizes them. Then, we introduce another objective InfoNCE Loss as follow:

$$\mathcal{L}\left(h_i, h_i^+, h_i^-\right) = -\log \frac{e^{sim\left(h_i, h_i^+\right)/\tau}}{e^{sim\left(h_i, h_i^+\right)/\tau} + \sum_{j=1}^{N-1} e^{sim\left(h_i, h_j^-\right)/\tau}}, \tag{2}$$

where h is the embedding of the sentence, $sim(:,:)$ represents the formula for calculating the semantic similarity between sentences, such as dot product, τ denotes the temperature coefficient to amplify the value of negative samples, and N stands for the number of samples in a training batch. This equation shows that if the vector of negative samples h_i^- is closer to the question vector h_i, the larger loss will be received by the equation.

Finally, we pick the optimal models from each of the two objective functions, and then fuse them to achieve better performance.

3 Experiment

3.1 Dataset

The validations are executed on a large-scale Chinese knowledge graph published by CCKS KBQA contest organizers, which contains 66.63 million triples, 25.59 million entities and nearly 400 thousand relations, with 6525 published raw training data, 2100 validation data and 1191 test data. In detail, each raw data has three pieces of information, namely question, SPARQL and answer. For example, given the question "What is the capital of Beethoven's country?", the SPARQL statement is "⟨Beethoven⟩ ⟨nationality⟩ ?y. ?y ⟨capital⟩ ?x.", and the answer is "⟨Paris⟩". This year, the knowledge base and questions in the field of life services are introduced on the basis of OpenKG. Meanwhile, questions from last year will be retained to train the models. Note that there are no answers in validation and test set, so we take 600 items from raw training set as the dev set to evaluate the performance of models. All experimental results in this paper are derived from the evaluations on dev set.

Table 4. Results about NER and EL.

Model	Recall@5
CRF	0.878
CRF + MRC	0.897
CRF + MRC + LAC	**0.924**

3.2   Processing of Training Data

Since each module in KERQA is trained individually for their own tasks, we have to process the raw data into the training data appropriate to their tasks. The training data in different modules will be elaborated in the following.

Question Classification. The classification model requires the output of a label for the given question. The label denotes the implicit structure of the question as described in Sect. 2.1. Thus, to determine the correct labels for the classification training data, we analyze the components of the SPARQL statement and design a program to annotate it. For example, for "⟨Beethoven⟩ ⟨nationality⟩ ?y. ?y ⟨capital⟩ ?x.", SPARQL statement has two triples and only 1 known entity, thus we consider it as a single-entity multi-hop structure (i.e. label-3).

Name Entity Recognition. Models in NER module call for a large amount of labeled training data. However, due to the prohibition of manual tags in this competition, we are prevented from obtaining the accurate NER training annotations. To solve this issue, we use the word-level matching between entity texts in SPARQL statements and spans in the question separated by split-word system (e.g. LAC) to retrieve spans (mentions) coming from question. Nevertheless, this operation may cause annotation failures and errors. Accordingly, we filter the questions without any labels and get about 5600 question and label pairs.

Path Ranking. The challenge in annotating the data for Path Ranking is to decide which path is the proper one. Our strategy is to compare all the known entities and relations in SPARQL and candidate paths. If they are identical, then we can deem this path to be the gold answer and annotate it as 1 while other paths are annotated as 0.

Note that, *Entity Linking* and *Path Generation* modules do not rely on training data. As we have accomplished the above operations, the models can be trained separately and we can choose the optimal models respectively.

3.3   Question Classification

We employ the MacBERT [4] BASE as our basic model and the parameters keep the settings of MacBERT [4] in this module. Furthermore, the following full

Table 5. Results on path ranking.

Model	F1
MacBERT	0.850
MacBERT (Triplet)	0.903
MacBERT (InfoNCE)	0.912
MacBERT (LCQMC + InfoNCE)	0.898
MacBERT (Triplet + InfoNCE)	**0.921**

connected layer converts a 768-dimensional vector into a 6-dimensional vector and we transform it into a probability distribution via a softmax layer. In the end, we choose the category with the highest probability as our classification label.

As we presented in Sect. 2.4, we use a coarse-grained way to get the classification label, enabling the accuracy of the task to improve from 91.7% to 94%.

3.4   Named Entity Recognition and Entity Linking

The absence of the precise labeling of NER forces us to use the recall rate of the entities extracted from SPARQL as our evaluation metric. Thus, we evaluate the integrated results of both NER and EL modules.

For NER module, we also utilized pretrained MacBERT in BERT+CRF and MRC models. BERT+CRF uses 12 layers MacBERT, while MRC uses 24 layers MacBERT (i.e. MacBERT LARGE). For EL module, we deploy the Elastic-Search system to search for entities in KG when given a mention, and then design a score equation to incorporate the degree information of the entities:

$$score = s + a * log(i + 1) + b * o, \tag{3}$$

where s is the default score for ES, indicating the text match between mention and entity, i denotes the in-degree of entities, o represents the out-degree of entities, a and b are hyper-parameters to make a trade-off between i and o. Eventually, we select the top 5 entities as candidates for each mention. Since ES does not require training, when we set a as 0.6 and b as 0.9, we can evaluate the performance of the NER module by the recall rate of the entities.

Experimental results are presented in Table 4. First, we observe that each component in NER makes a contribution to improving the recall rate. Second, the result proves the usefulness of LAC for unexpected mentions, as discussed in Sect. 2.2. Third, the integration of the two modules obtains a 92.4% recall rate, which fully demonstrates the effectiveness of ES in tackling EL tasks.

3.5   Path Generation

In the *Path Generation* module, the templates suffer from the long-tail problem, i.e. a small part of the template covers the majority of the questions. Thus, in

Table 6. Overall results on test dataset.

Team	Test (F1)
MiQa	**0.78855**
Future-Aware (**Ours**)	0.78789
xitongzhishenyuwotongzai	0.78517
fangtazhidui	0.76366

order to reduce the number of candidate paths and improve the efficiency in inference phase, we discard many complex templates such as 3-hop template. The coverage rate of the templates in training set hits 95.5%.

3.6 Path Ranking

Table 5 shows ranking accuracy in terms of F1 score for the dev set. We have the following observations.

First, models optimized by Triplet and InfoNCE losses outperform the MacBERT BASE model by up to 90.3 and 91.2% of F1 score, respectively. This implies that these losses indeed alleviate the long-tail problem, as concluded in Sect. 2.5. Second, InfoNCE is slightly superior to Triplet by up to 0.9% improvement of F1 score. It shows that simply using the Euclidean distance is inadequate for semi-hard and hard data. Accordingly, we use InfoNCE to give these data a larger penalty. Third, An external dataset LCQMC is harmful in this task according to the result. We hypothesize that the distribution of data in this competition is quite different from that of LCQMC. Finally, the fusion of models is applied to this task and achieves the best performance.

3.7 Overall Result

We conducted numerous experiments on test dataset and had obtained a competitive score 78.789%, which ranked second in this competition (the first place was only 0.07% higher than ours). According to Table 6, we notice that the gap between the top three scores is extremely small. Therefore, we can hardly conclude that one of these proposed methods is superior to others. Moreover, there still has huge room for improvement, as the highest score is merely 78.8855%. More creative and effective solutions are badly in need to address this task.

4   Conclusion

In this paper, we proposed a novel Knowledge-Enhanced Retrieval Question Answering (KERQA) framework to precisely extract gold answers from a large-scale knowledge graph. Specifically, five modules were designed and integrated to handle the complicated questions with remarkable performance, namely question classification, named entity recognition, entity linking, path generation and path ranking. Extensive validations have demonstrated the effectiveness of our KERQA framework, which achieved an F1 score of 78.78% on the final leaderboard of CCKS 2021 KBQA contest.

Acknowledgements. This research was partially supported by grants from the National Key Research and Development Program of China (Grant No.2018YFB 1402600), and the National Natural Science Foundation of China (Grant No.62072423).

References

1. Li, X., Feng, J., Meng, Y., Han, Q., Wu, F., Li, J.: A unified MRC framework for named entity recognition. In: Proceedings of the 58th Annual Meeting of the Association for Computational Linguistics, pp. 5849–5859. Association for Computational Linguistics, Online (2020). https://doi.org/10.18653/v1/2020.acl-main.519

2. Yan, Y., Li, R., Wang, S., Zhang, F., Wu, W., Xu, W.: ConSERT: a contrastive framework for self-supervised sentence representation transfer. In: Proceedings of the 59th Annual Meeting of the Association for Computational Linguistics and the 11th International Joint Conference on Natural Language Processing (Volume 1: Long Papers), pp. 5065–5075. Association for Computational Linguistics, Online (2021). https://doi.org/10.18653/v1/2021.acl-long.393

3. Oord, A. van den, Li, Y., Vinyals, O.: Representation Learning with Contrastive Predictive Coding. arXiv:1807.03748 [cs, stat] (2019)

4. Cui, Y., Che, W., Liu, T., Qin, B., Wang, S., Hu, G.: Revisiting pre-trained models for chinese natural language processing. In: Findings of the Association for Computational Linguistics: EMNLP 2020, pp. 657–668 (2020). https://doi.org/10.18653/v1/2020.findings-emnlp.58

5. Abujabal, A., Yahya, M., Riedewald, M., Weikum, G.: Automated template generation for question answering over knowledge graphs. In: Proceedings of the 26th International Conference on World Wide Web, Perth, Australia, pp. 1191–1200. International World Wide Web Conferences Steering Committee (2017). https://doi.org/10.1145/3038912.3052583

6. Zheng, W., Yu, J.X., Zou, L., Cheng, H.: Question answering over knowledge graphs: question understanding via template decomposition. Proc. VLDB Endow. **11**, 1373–1386 (2018). https://doi.org/10.14778/3236187.3236192

7. Yao, X., Van Durme, B.: Information extraction over structured data: question answering with freebase. In: Proceedings of the 52nd Annual Meeting of the Association for Computational Linguistics (Volume 1: Long Papers), Baltimore, Maryland, pp. 956–966. Association for Computational Linguistics (2014). https://doi.org/10.3115/v1/P14-1090

8. Lai, Y., Feng, Y., Yu, X., Wang, Z., Xu, K., Zhao, D.: Lattice CNNs for Matching Based Chinese Question Answering. arXiv:1902.09087 [cs] (2019)

9. Xu, K., Reddy, S., Feng, Y., Huang, S., Zhao, D.: Question Answering on Freebase via Relation Extraction and Textual Evidence. arXiv:1603.00957 [cs] (2016)

10. Berant, J., Liang, P.: Semantic parsing via paraphrasing. In: Proceedings of the 52nd Annual Meeting of the Association for Computational Linguistics (Volume 1: Long Papers), Baltimore, Maryland, pp. 1415–1425. Association for Computational Linguistics (2014). https://doi.org/10.3115/v1/P14-1133

Multi-label Fine-Grained Entity Typing for Baidu Wikipedia Based on Pre-trained Model

Keyu Pu, Hongyi Liu, Yixiao Yang[✉], Wenyi Lv, and Jinlong Li

China Merchants Bank Artificial Intelligence Laboratory, ShenZhen 518000, China

Abstract. It is a crucial premise for named entity recognition task to achieve high-accuracy entity extraction. CCKS-2021 held a Knowledge Graph Fine-grained Entity Typing competition, and 262 teams participated. What is challenging in the task is the extremely large amounts of unlabeled data and the multi-label entity typing. In our approach, a semi-supervised learning strategy is conducted to cope with the unlabeled data, and a multi-label loss is employed to recognize the multi-label entity. An F1-score of 0.85498 on the final testing data is achieved, which verifies the performance of our approach, and ranks the second place in the task.

Keywords: Fine-grained entity typing · Multi-label · Unlabeled data

1 Introduction

Named entity recognition (NER) task (first proposed in MUC-6) is a subtask of information extraction that seeks to locate named entities in the unstructured text, and classify the entities into pre-defined types (also known as entity typing) such as person, location, organization, etc. [1–3]. As an important basic work in the field of Natural Language Processing (NLP), the accuracy of NER affects many downstream tasks, such as information extraction, question answering, machine translation, etc.

However, traditional coarse-grained entity typing is not accurate enough for many actual tasks. An example of a question answering task is shown in Table 1. It is not enough to answer the question in the first row when only knowing three candidates in the second row belongs to the person type. The person type needs to be subdivided into different occupation type. In addition to the smaller category scale, the number of types is also increasing, which has reached dozens or even hundreds because of the existing large-scale database and knowledge graph. Besides, acquiring the hierarchical relationship among entity types is also needed in some certain tasks. In this case, coarse-grained entity typing will not only increase the difficulty of manual labeling, but also affects the processing quality of many downstream work such as relation extraction and event extraction. Therefore, in order to meet the needs of increasingly complex NLP application scenario, current trends are to develop fine-grained entity typing (FET).

B. Qin et al. (Eds.): CCKS 2021, CCIS 1553, pp. 114–123, 2022.
https://doi.org/10.1007/978-981-19-0713-5_13

Table 1. An illustration of a question answering task.

Question	Who is the author of *Romance of the Three Kingdoms*?		
Answer candidates	Guanzhong Luo	Ming Yao	Jackie Chen
Coarse-grained entity typing	Person	Person	Person
Fine-grained entity typing	Person/Author	Person/Athlete	Person/Actor

FET is a challenging task that aims to classify entities into a large set of fine-grained sub-types. As shown in Fig. 1, a FET task may contain several dozens of types that are arranged into a hierarchical structure, and one entity may belong to multiple types (multi-label entity). Compared to the coarse-grained entity typing, FET provides more semantic information for other NLP tasks, which helps to improve the efficiency and accuracy of question answering system, entity recommendation and other downstream tasks.

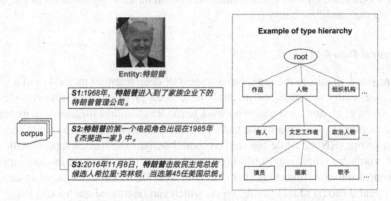

Fig. 1. An illustration of the fine-grained entity typing

The FET task was first proposed in 2006 [4], and the focus of which was mainly on how to design manual features. However, the manual features were extremely complicated to design and were hard to migrate to other tasks, so the early research developed slowly. Thanks to the development of deep learning and its powerful representation capabilities, FET has also developed to a great extent. Due to the increase of entity type amount, the demand for manually annotate data has increased dramatically, which brings great cost. Therefore, how to improve the classification accuracy with low cost remains unsolved.

In this paper, a FET method, resolving two challenging problems: extremely large amounts of unlabeled data and multi-label entity typing, is proposed. Our approach achieves an F1-score of 0.85498, which ranks the second place among 262 participating teams in the CCKS-2021 Knowledge Graph Fine-grained Entity Typing Task.

This paper is structured as follows. The related work of the FET task is briefly introduced in Sect. 2. The principle of our method is presented in Sect. 3. The experimental results are exhibited in Sect. 4. Section 5 summarizes this paper.

2   Related Work

Fine-grained entity typing has been widely studied in recent years. Previous FET methods can be categorized into three groups: machine learning based methods, neural based methods, and attention based methods.

2.1   Machine Learning Based Methods

Lee et al. first studied the fine-grained entity typing task. They extended the coarse-grained type of named entity to 147 types to improve the performance of question answering system [4]. Conditional Random Field (CRF) was also applied to detect the boundary of named entities [5]. In addition, Maximum Entropy Model was employed to classify the candidate entity [6].

2.2   Neural Based Methods

In recent years, thanks to the rapid development of deep learning methods and artificial intelligence, many neural-based methods have been proposed and achieved pleasant results. Dong et al. first used neural network to model candidate mention and its context [7]. The mention model obtains the vector representations of entities by using recursive neural network (RNN), while the context model derives the hidden representations of context words by employing multi-layer perceptron. Then the vectors and input are concatenated into a softmax classifier [8]. After that, Karn et al. introduced an encoder-decoder neural model to infer entity types, which can be trained end-to-end [9].

2.3   Pre-trained Based Methods

Recently, substantial works have shown that pre-trained models (PTMs) on the large corpus can learn universal language representations, which are beneficial for downstream NLP tasks and can avoid training a new model from scratch. Very deep PTMs have shown their powerful abilities in learning universal language representations, the representative work of which are BERT (Bidirectional Encoder Representation from Transformer) [10] and OpenAI GPT (Generative Pre-training) [11]. Since BERT, fine-tuning has become a mainstream approach to adapt PTMs for the downstream tasks including fine-grained entity typing. How to combine PTMs with fine-grained entity typing is the focus of this paper.

3   Approach

The processing flow of our approach is illustrated in Fig. 2 below.

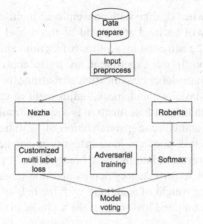

Fig. 2. The processing flow of the approach

3.1 Data Preparation

To overcome the challenge of not providing labeled data, 2000 pieces of data are randomly selected for manual labeling to train the initial model.

3.2 Input Preprocess

The randomly selected data uses the name, title, abstract and keyword concatenate as the original features input of the neural network model. 474 important keywords were selected as the input features of the model.

3.3 Overall Model Structure

The model used for classification contains two different structures. One is a multi-label classification model based on NEZHA and customized multi-label loss function, and the other is a multi-classification model based on Roberta and softmax cross entropy.

3.4 Multi-label Classification

BERT incorporates an absolute positional encoding for each position to initialize a position embedding which is learned via pre-training [12], while NEZHA employ functional relative positional encoding through a fixed sinusoidal function [13]. The advantage of using a fixed sinusoidal function is that it can extrapolate the model to a longer sequence length than the length encountered in training [13]. A more effective whole word masking strategy was used in the NEZHA model to replace random masking for training BERT [13]. NEZHA also elevated training speed by 2–3 times through a mixed intensive reading training technology, and reduced the space consumption of the model, which means a larger batch can be used in the pretraining process [13]. In addition, A lamb optimizer was employed to greatly reduce the pretraining time [13].

Generally speaking, when dealing with conventional multi-classification problems, a full connection layer will be used at the end of the model to output the score of each class, and then will be activated by a softmax function, and the cross entropy will be set as the loss function. In our experiment, we try to apply the "softmax + cross entropy" scheme to the multi-label classification scenario, expecting to get the loss of multi-label classification tasks without special adjustment of the class weight and the threshold. Customized multi-label loss function is a special multi-label loss calculated method, and the natural and concise generalization of "softmax + cross entropy" in multi-label classification task does not have category imbalance, because it does not turn the multi-label classification into multiple binary classification problems, but into a pairwise comparison of target category scores and non-target category scores, and automatically balances the weight of each item with the help of the good properties of logsumexp. Formula 1 is a unified loss form of the multi-label classification.

$$\log\left(1 + \sum_{i\in\Omega neg,\ j\in\Omega pos} e^{si-sj} + \sum_{i\in\Omega neg} e^{si-s0} + \sum_{j\in\Omega pos} e^{s0-sj}\right)$$
$$= \log\left(e^{s0} + \sum_{i\in\Omega neg} e^{si}\right) + \log\left(e^{-s0} + \sum_{j\in\Omega pos} e^{-sj}\right)$$

(1)

3.5 Multi-classification

An enhanced version of Bert and a more refined tuning version of Bert model (RoBERTa) was proposed in 2019 [14]. The RoBERTa model made progress on the previously proposed Bert in three aspects. First, the optimization parameters of BERT were tuned when training the RoBERTa. Second, the training strategy was improved by removing the NSP (next sentence prediction) loss, which was able to match or slightly improves downstream task performance, and a larger batch size was applied in the RoBERTa. Third, on the data level, BPE (byte pair encoding) was used to process the text data, and a larger data set was employed in the RoBERTa.

BPE coding scheme is a mixture of the character level and the word level representation, which can deal with a large number of common words in natural language corpus. BPE does not rely on complete words, but on sub word units. These sub word units are extracted through statistical analysis of the training corpus, and their word table size is usually between 10000 and 100000. When modeling a large and diverse corpus, Unicode characters occupy most of the vocabulary, but BPE uses byte pairs rather than Unicode characters as sub word units.

In the last layer of the neural network, the softmax function is usually used to compress the output of each neuron between [0,1]. The cross entropy constructed is used as the loss function. Formula 2 is used to describe the mathematical expression of cross entropy loss.

$$H(p,q) = -\sum_{i=1}^{n} p(xi)\ln(q(xi))$$

(2)

3.6 Adversarial Training

Model fusion adopts multi-model voting attenuation strategy and FGM adversarial training to improve the robustness of the model. In the process of adversarial training, the samples will be mixed with some small disturbances (the change is very small, but it is likely to cause misclassification), and then make the neural network adapt to this change, so as to be robust to the adversarial samples. In our experiment, the embedding parameter matrix is directly disturbed to obtain the diversity of samples, as shown in the Fig. 3 below.

Based on the first version of the model, combined with the correction algorithm, the data is increased to the amount of 4000. In order to solve the problem that the text of entity description is too long, the summary is extracted by textrank algorithm and then put it into the model.

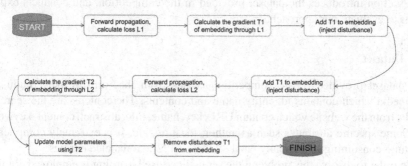

Fig. 3. Adversarial training process based on embedding disturbance

3.7 Model Voting

According to the idea of ensemble learning, the output results of different models will be voted by the bagging strategy based on the weight calculation. First, make statistics on all predictions and aggregate the prediction results of all predictors. For classification scenarios, the principle of the minority obeying the majority can be utilized to calculate the final results or calculate the average prediction probability of all categories. Then, make horizontal comparison in the direction of categories, and directly calculate the average in regression scenarios. Compared with the single model scenario, this integration mode can effectively reduce the deviation and variance. The structure of the multi-model voting strategy based on the ensemble learning is shown in the Fig. 4 below.

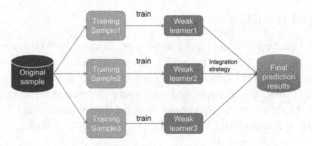

Fig. 4. The structure of the multi-model voting strategy

4 Experiment

This section introduces the dataset provided in the competition, and conducts experiments to evaluate our approach.

4.1 Dataset

The dataset provided in the competition comes from the website likes Baidu and Wikipedia which contains id, entity name and contents. The contents are the searched results from the website which contain URL, key, name, title, abstract, content, keywords and some specific attributes such as author, location, etc. It is extremely complicated and time-consuming to manually label all these 612269 unlabeled entities.

In order to resolve this problem, the semi-supervised learning is employed. At first, we annotate 2000 entities manually and use these labeled data to train a classifier. In the second step, the classifier is applied to the unlabeled data to acquire label with class probabilities. In the third step, the correct entities predicted is chosen to iterate the classifier, until that we get 4000 high qualities labeled entities.

As shown in Table 2, there are overall 55 labels in the dataset, which contain the label named "other" indicating that the entity is not among these labels provided officially. The FET task is a multi-label entity recognition task, which means the entity perhaps has more than one label. In the training dataset, there are 185 multi-label entities in total.

4.2 Implementation

Two pre-trained models are chosen in our method, one of which is the NEZHA-LARGE-WWM which includes functional relative positional encoding as an effective positional encoding scheme, whole word masking strategy, mixed precision training and the LAMB optimizer in training the models [13], the other of which is the RoBERTa-LARGE which is a robustly optimized BERT pretraining approach [14]. We apply Dropout to the output of the pre-trained model with the rate set to 0.1. During the training process, we set the batch size as 2, the learning rate as $2e-5$ and the epoch number as 15. Furthermore, we apply adversarial training to improve robustness. In our approach, the NEZHA-LARGE-WWM is used to build our multi-label classification model and the RoBERTa-LARGE is used to build our single-label classification model.

Table 2. Training dataset partition

Category	Total	Category	Total
Person	11	Location	52
Person > artist	21	Location > residence	151
Person > artist > author	88	Location > infrastructure	296
Person > artist > screenwriter	70	Location > natural scenery	95
Person > artist > singer	71	Location > tourist attraction	54
Person > artist > actor	148	Location > sphere	47
Person > artist > dancer	6	Production	10
Person > artist > director	72	Production > TV production	19
Person > artist > photographer	19	Production > TV production > movie	280
Person > artist > poet	20	Production > TV production > TV drama	128
Person > artist > painter	51	Production > TV production > cartoon	52
Person > athlete	21	Production > TV production > TV show	26
Person > athlete > football player	67	Production > written work	48
Person > athlete > basketball player	10	Production > written work > book	103
Person > athlete > diver	6	Production > written work > fiction	182
Person > athlete > track man	9	Production > written work > poetry	110
Person > athlete > swimmer	13	Production > written work > comic	82
Person > athlete > gymnast	12	Production > written work > opera and drama	8
Person > merchant	20	Production > written work > Article	93
Person > teacher	210	Production > musical work	1
Person > doctor	27	Production > musical work > song	86
Person > politician	113	Production > musical work > album	70
Person > lawyer	13	Production > software	8
Person > journalist	12	Production > software > game	138
Person > virtual character	124	Organization	56
Organization > government	213	Organization > company	303
Organization > educational institution	151	Organization > band	17
Other	111		

For our model ensemble strategy, 8 single-label classification models and 8 multi-label classification models has been trained. We ensemble the 8 single-label predictions to get the single-label results and then ensemble the 8 multi-label predictions. Finally, we combine these two results by choosing the single-label records in the single-label results and the multi-label records in the multi-label results.

4.3 Main Result

Since we can only get the score of the validation data on the leader board daily, we conduct experiments on the validation data. The F1-score on validation data is 0.83447 which is the highest score in the leader board daily of the competition. Finally, the F1-score of our approach on the final testing data is 0.85498 which ranks the second place.

4.4 Ablation Study

We conduct an ablation study during the competition where the results are shown in Table 3. We have two baseline models. One is built for predicting only the single-label entity which could predict only one label even if the entity has more than 1 tag. Another is built for predicting multi-label entity which is also very effective on single-label entity. These two models use both the entity name and the abstract as the input, acquire the F1-score: 74.952% and 75.024%. Actually, there are many meaningful attributes for each entity in the dataset such as keywords, title, content. We add these attributes as input as well, and get the better scores which indicates that these features improve the classification performance. It is worth mentioning that the explanation of the entity named "content" is complex and extremely long, and we propose two solutions to deal with it: set the max length of content as 340, use the summary of content got by Text-Rank. The results

Table 3. Results on the validation dataset

Method	F1 (%)
Baseline single-label	74.952
w/Keywords	78.493
w/Title	79.269
w/content (max length 340)	80.498
w/content (summary)	**81.091**
Baseline multi-label	75.024
w/Keywords	78.896
w/Title	79.316
w/content (max length 340)	81.411
w/content (summary)	**81.802**
Ensemble strategy	**83.447**

of these two solutions show that learning entity typing with its explanation is effective. Finally, 1.6% improvement on the score of the final result is achieved by our model ensemble strategy.

5 Conclusion

An entity typing approach which fully utilizes all the data comes from the website is proposed in this paper. The semi-supervised learning is used to resolve the first challenge: extremely large amounts of unlabeled data, and the multi-label loss is used to resolve another challenge: multi-label entity recognition. The experimental results show that our approach achieves a great performance (F1-score: 0.85498) and ranks the second place in the CCKS-2021 Knowledge Graph Fine-grained Entity Typing competition.

References

1. Chinchor, N.: MUC-6 named entity task definition (version 2.1). In: Proceedings of the 6th Conference on Message Understanding, Columbia, Maryland (1995)
2. Chinchor, N., Robinson, P.: MUC-7 named entity task definition. In: Proceedings of the 7th Conference on Message Understanding (1997)
3. Wikipedia. https://en.wikipedia.org/w/index.php?title=Named-entity_recognition&oldid= 1040289513. Accessed 16 Sept 2021
4. Lee, C., et al.: Fine-grained named entity recognition using conditional random fields for question answering. In: Ng, H.T., Leong, M.-K., Kan, M.-Y., Ji, D. (eds.) AIRS 2006. LNCS, vol. 4182, pp. 581–587. Springer, Heidelberg (2006). https://doi.org/10.1007/11880592_49
5. Mintz, M., Bills, S., Snow, R., Jurafsky, D.: Distant supervision for relation extraction without labeled data. In: Proceedings of the Joint Conference of the 47th Annual Meeting of the ACL and the 4th International Joint Conference on Natural Language Processing of the AFNLP, pp. 1003–1011 (2009)
6. Yosef, M.A., Bauer, S., Hoffart, J., Saniol, M., Weikum, G.: Hyena: hierarchical type classification for entity names. In: Proceedings of COLING 2012, pp.1361–1370 (2012)
7. Dong, L., Wei, F., Sun, H., Zhou, M.l., Xu, K.: A hybrid neural model for type classification of entity mentions. In: Proceedings of the Twenty-Fourth International Joint Conference on Artificial Intelligence (IJCAI 2015), pp.1243–1249. AAAI Press (2015)
8. Berger, A., Della Pietra, S.A., Della Pietra, V.J.: A maximum entropy approach to natural language processing. In: Computational Linguistics, pp. 39–71 (1996)
9. Karn, S., Waltinger, U., Schütze, H.: End-to-end trainable attentive decoder for hierarchical entity classification. In: Association for Computational Linguistics, Valencia, pp. 752–758 (2017)
10. Devlin, J., Chang, M.-W., Lee, K., Toutanova, K.: BERT: pre-training of deep bidirectional transformers for language understanding. In: NAACL-HLT (2019)
11. Radford, A., Narasimhan, K., Salimans, T., Sutskever, I.: Improving language understanding by generative pre-training (2018)
12. Vaswani, A., et al.: Attention is all you need. In: Advances in Neural Information Processing Systems, pp. 5998–6008 (2017)
13. Wei, J., et al.: NEZHA: Neural Contextualized Representation for Chinese Language Understanding. arXiv preprint. arXiv:1909.00204 (2019)
14. Liu, Y.: RoBERTa: a robustly optimized BERT pretraining approach. arXiv preprint. arXiv: 1907.11692 (2019)

Multi-strategies Integrated Information Extraction for Scholar Profiling Task

Jian Li[1]([✉]), Ting Zhang[1], Yali Wang[1], Hongguan Gui[2], Xin Tan[2], and Zihao Wang[2]

[1] PLA Strategic Support Force Information Engineering University, Luoyang 471003, Henan, China

[2] Data Grand Information Technology (Shanghai) Co., Ltd., Shanghai 201203, China

Abstract. Although the traditional information extraction tasks with labeled data sets are convenient for model design and training, they are also limited by the labeled data sets. In contrast, information extraction directly oriented to web search results is more flexible, practical and challenging. The evaluation task of *CCKS*-2021 "Aminer Scholar Profiling" requires accurate extraction of character attributes in the limited search range. A group of web information extraction methods based on multi-strategies integration are proposed for the task: (1) give priority to extracting attributes from semi-structured web page tags, otherwise try to mine from unstructured webpage text; (2) transform the unstructured attribute extraction tasks into text classification tasks, and construct training data sets for them respectively; (3) design a special OCR method to recognize the text attributes embedded in the images. Using the above strategies and methods, the accuracy in the validation set and test set reached 75.68 and 74.84 respectively, and finally won the first place in this evaluation task. When deep learning algorithms develop to a relatively mature stage on some specific tasks, taking advantage of the characteristics of the business and pre-processing of the data are more effective than tuning of the model.

Keywords: Scholar profiling · Information extraction · Text classification · OCR

1 Introduction

The advent of the big data era and the latest round of progress in artificial intelligence have largely benefited from the development of web technology. Compared with sensors in the Internet of Things, the big data comes more from various web applications. At present, artificial intelligence has developed to the stage of deep learning and has been widely used in many areas [1]. Computing power, algorithms and calculation data are called the three essential factors of deep learning. In a narrow sense, calculation data can be regarded as various task datasets which also mainly come from the web.

Natural language processing (NLP) is known as the pearl on the crown of artificial intelligence, and information extraction is one of the most important tasks in the field of NLP. Traditional information extraction tasks are usually provided with labeled data sets, which is convenient for model design and training, but is also restricted by the labeled

© Springer Nature Singapore Pte Ltd. 2022
B. Qin et al. (Eds.): CCKS 2021, CCIS 1553, pp. 124–132, 2022.
https://doi.org/10.1007/978-981-19-0713-5_14

data sets. In contrast, information extraction directly oriented to web search results is more flexible, practical and challenging. The "Aminer Scholar Profiling" in *CCKS*-2021[1] belongs to this kind of evaluation task, which is carried out based on the *Biendata* competition platform [2]. This task aims to extract, label and statistically analyze the accurate factual knowledge of experts and scholars from the web page, which can be used in academic search, scientific research services, talent mining and other aspects in order to promote the development of academic artificial intelligence and scientific & technological information analysis system [3].

The authors have participated in the above evaluation task, proposed a group of information extraction methods based on multi-strategies integration, and achieved excellent results. This paper will introduce the task, methods and experimental results in details.

2 Task

CCKS-2021 "Aminer Scholar Profiling" evaluation task data set contains about 10000 scholar profiling samples. About 6000 of them include all fields such as name, organization, home page, professional title, email, gender, language and avatar, which can be used as training data. The remaining samples only give the name and organization fields as verification data and test data respectively (half each). In addition, the evaluation task provides each scholar with a group of web pages returned by the search engine, including Google search result list pages (up to 2) and the corresponding content pages (up to 20). Participants need to extract the attribute information of scholars from this group of web pages. There are two important restrictions on the evaluation task: (1) only the given pages and the links in them can be visited, and deeper links or other webpages are denied; (2) only the given labelled data can be used to train the model, and any additional labelled data can not be used.

Information extraction for web data mainly includes two categories, which are based on webpage structure and open text respectively. The former uses the tree structure of DOM document to locate elements (markup nodes), and usually takes the internal text or attribute value of the element as the extraction target. This method has high accuracy and mature technology, but the extraction conditions are relatively harsh. It requires good webpage structure, clear extraction target location, and multiple extraction templates for different webpage frameworks.

For the information that is difficult to locate clearly in the webpage, it is necessary to extract from the open text of the webpage with the NLP technology. The text in the webpage is very complex. We usually select the text related to the topic such as title, body and comment, and filter out the navigation menu at the top, the copyright notice at the bottom and the advertising links on both sides. Based on the above text data, we can transform the information extraction task into specific NLP tasks (such as text classification, entity recognition, relationship extraction, etc.).

Text classification is the most basic and important task in NLP field. It is often used in emotion analysis, news classification, text inference, Q&A judgment and so on. Text classification can be roughly divided into shallow learning methods and deep learning

---

[1] *CCKS*-2021: the 15th China Conference on Knowledge Graph and Semantic Computing (http://sigkg.cn/ccks2021/).

methods [4]. The former are mainly based on statistical models, such as naive Bayes [5], nearest neighbor (KNN [6]), support vector machine (SVM [7]). The latter are mainly based on various deep neural networks, including recurrent neural networks (Tree-LSTM [8], MT-LSTM [9]), convolutional neural networks (TextCNN [10], HFT-CNN [11]), graph neural networks (DGCNN [12], TextGCN [13]), pre-training language models (Bert [14], XLNet [15]) and others.

Statistical analysis of this evaluation task shows that about a third of scholars' Google search results include their Aminer page, in which all the target attributes can be clearly located. Therefore, we will extract attributes from semi-structured web page data if the search results include the Aminer page for a given scholar, otherwise we will use NLP technology to extract attributes from unstructured open text.

3   Methods

3.1   Extracting Information from Semi-structured Data

For those scholars whose Aminer page is included in Google search results, we can directly load the web page and extract the attributes. The attributes displayed on the web page include avatar, homepage, email, etc. (see Fig. 1).

Fig. 1. A scholar page in Aminer.

In practice, we use the 3rd-party Python library *selenium.webdriver* to run the *Firefox* browser to load the webpage, and then locate the target elements through XPath. The XPath values of the target elements are shown in Table 1.

Other attributes of scholars (such as gender, title and language) can be extracted from the webpage source code (as shown in Fig. 2, the highlighted part is the "gender" of the scholar).

In practice, we obtain the above 3 attribute values through regular expression matching, and the specific expressions are shown as Table 2. The attribute value should be the matching part of ".*?".

Table 1. XPath of the target elements.

Attribute name	XPath	Target	Attribute value
avatar	//img[@class='avatar']	<img>	src attribute of <img>
homepage	//a[@class='homepage baseInfo'	<a>	href attribute of <a>
email	//p[@class='email info_line']/img	<img>	text on <img>

Fig. 2. Source code of Aminer scholar page.

Table 2. Regular expression of the target elements.

Attribute name	Regular expression
gender	"gender":".*?"
language	"lang":".*?"
title	"position":".*?","position_zh"

3.2 Recognize Text in Pictures

It should be noted that the "email" attribute in the Aminer page has a special form. It is not expressed in the form of text but embedded in a picture (see Fig. 3). We have tried to invoke *Baidu OCR API* to recognize the characters in these pictures, but the recognition accuracy is too low to be exploited.

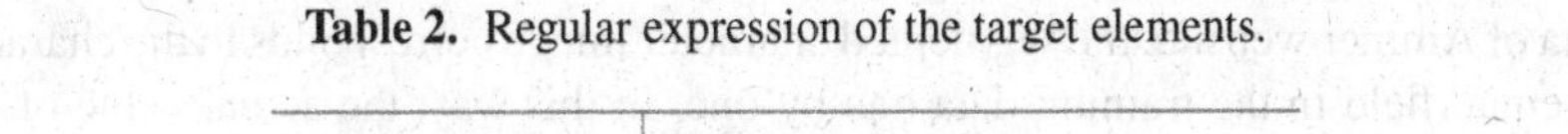

rboutaba@uwaterloo.ca;cs-director@uwaterloo.ca

Fig. 3. An image with email attribute in the Aminer page.

Statistical analysis shows that the characters in the email address are very limited, mainly including English letters, numbers and some special symbols, with a total of more than 60 characters. If each character can be recognized, we will get the complete email address.

We first need to cut each character in the picture into a small image. The height of the original picture is 24 pixels and the length is variable (related to the number of characters). There is at least one pixel space between adjacent characters, by which we can segment the original picture. Since the width of each character is different (for example, i is thinner than w), we uniformly set the width of a single character image to 10 pixels. That is, a character is represented by an image with a size of 10 * 24. The characters are displayed from the first column on the left, and the redundant parts on the right are all set to white (see Fig. 4).

X   @

Fig. 4. Characters cut from email pictures.

As for character image recognition, we had considered a scheme: segment and count the characters in all email pictures, save different characters as separate pictures, and then label them manually. Because the number of characters is a little bit more than 60, the labelling workload is very small. It is really a practical and feasible scheme.

However, this evaluation task requires that no additional labelled data can be used (strictly speaking, even labelling only dozens of characters is not allowed), so we propose another scheme of automatic labelling. Assuming that the training data is consistent with the data of Aminer website, the segmented character image corresponds to the characters in the email field in the training data one by one. In this way, the actual value of each character picture can be automatically labelled according to training data. The statistical results are stored in a dictionary structure (see Fig. 5). The key of the dictionary is a "0/1" string with a length of 240 (representing a binary image with a size of 10 * 24), and the value is the corresponding actual character. Using this dictionary, the email attributes can be recognized easily.

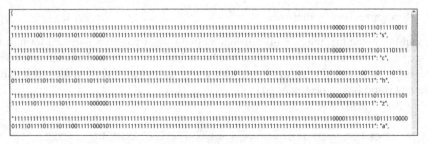

Fig. 5. Serialization results of the "character image" dictionary.

3.3 Extracting Information from Unstructured Data

For those scholars whose Aminer pages are not included in the search results, we will extract their target attributes from the open text of the webpages. Judging the gender of scholars can be regarded as a binary classification problem. The value range of professional titles is a finite set, which is equivalent to a multi classification problem. Judging scholars' language is similar to their professional titles, which also can be considered as a multi classification problem. Since scholars' home pages are only selected from the search results, determining whether a URL is the homepage of a given person is essentially a binary classification problem. We can first match all the email addresses in the relevant webpages and then determine whether an email belongs to a given person, which is also a binary classification problem. In this way, each attribute extraction can be transformed to a classification problem.

We adopt the deep learning method to extract the attributes of the professional title, language and homepage. As to the homepage attribute, we constructed training data for "judging whether a link is the homepage of a given scholar" (see Fig. 6). Each row of training data represents a sample, where the content includes name, organization, website address and page summary, and the label indicates whether it is the homepage (0 for "No", 1 for "Yes"). Similar methods are used for the title and language attributes, but the training samples are different. In the "Title Classification" training data, the sample content includes the name, organization and page summary containing keywords of the professional title, and the sample label is the number corresponding to the title. In the "language classification" training data, the sample content includes the name, organization and page summary containing keywords of language or country, and the sample label is the number corresponding to the language. Bert + Softmax classification models will be trained with the above data sets.

```
name: Michael Auli; org: Facebook AI Research; https://michaelauli.github.io/; I am a Research Scientist at Facebook AI Research in Menlo Park,
CA and I work on machine learning, natural language processing and speech recognition.;    1
name: Michael Auli; org: Facebook AI Research; https://icml.cc/Conferences/2017/ScheduleMultitrack?event=806; Jonas Gehring · Michael Auli ·
David Grangier - Denis Yarats - Yann Dauphin. Wed Aug 09 01:30 AM -- 05:00 AM ... Jonas Gehring (Facebook AI Research) ...;    0
name: Michael Auli; org: Facebook AI Research; https://dl.acm.org/profile/99659338361; Convolutional sequence to sequence learning · Jonas
Gehring. Facebook AI Research. .; Michael Auli. Facebook AI Research. .; David Grangier. Facebook AI ...;    0
name: Pieter Colpaert; org: Ghent University; https://pietercolpaert.be/; Pieter Colpaert. Postdoctoral researcher public Web APIs at Ghent
University– IDLab– imec ... If you are nearby Ghent, I am always up for a cup of coffee.;    1
name: Pieter Colpaert; org: Ghent University; https://github.com/OpenTransport/StopTimes; Stop Times vocabulary. Editors. Pieter Colpaert (Open
Knowledge | iMinds - Ghent University - MultiMedia Lab); Andrew Byrd (Conveyal) ...;    0
name: Tim Salcudean; org: University of British Columbia; https://www.ece.ubc.ca/~tims/; C.A. Laszlo Chair of Biomedical Engineering and Canada
Research Chair, P. Eng., FCAE, FIEEE B. Eng. ('79), M. Eng. ('81), McGill University Ph.D. ('86) ...;    1
```

Fig. 6. Training data of "homepage classification".

Gender and email attributes are judged by statistical methods. The gender judgment process is as follows: segment the text in the scholar's relevant webpages into words and count the number of gender feature words (see Table 3). If there are more female feature words than male, it will be judged as a woman, otherwise a man.

Table 3. Feature words of Gender

Gender	Feature words
Male	he, him, his, boy, Mr., Sir, ...
Female	she, her, girl, Mrs., Ms., Miss, Madam, ...

For the email attribute, we first extract all the legal email addresses in the relevant webpages using regular expressions, and then judge whether each email belongs to the given scholar. People usually register email accounts with their own names or abbreviations, so we assume that the registered email names (the part before @) are similar to the real names in probability. For example, Ravinder Dahiya's email is *"Ravinder.Dahiya@glasgow.ac.uk"*, in which the real name is almost identical to the registered name. For another example, Hamid Gharavi's email address is *"hgharavi@derainsgharavi.com"*, in which the similarity is also very high. We use Jaccard index to express the similarity of two strings. The calculation formula is as follows:

$$\text{Sim\_Jaccard}(r\_name, e\_name) = \frac{\text{len}(\text{set}(r\_name) \cap \text{set}(e\_name))}{\text{len}(\text{set}(r\_name) \cup \text{set}(e\_name))}$$

In the above formula, *r_name* means the real name of the scholar, *e_name* refers to the registered name of the email. The calculation process is as follows: convert the two strings into character sets (ignoring case), and then divide the number of elements in the intersection of the two sets by the number of elements in the union set. In practice, we set the Jaccard similarity threshold to 0.3.

4   Experiments

4.1   Data Distribution

The statistical distribution of attributes in the training dataset are elaborated to verify the proposed methods more accurately. The statistical results are as follows: 89.7% of the scholars in the training set are men. Among these scholars, 41.9% speak Chinese, 33.7% speak English, and the rest speak other or unknown languages. The proportion of scholars with titles of "Professor", "researcher" and "associate professor" is 68.8%, 5.9% and 4.3% respectively, and the rest have other titles or no_titles. 20.1% of the scholars have no homepage, and the rest have at least one homepage. 19.6% of the scholars have no email, and the rest have at least one email address.

It can be seen that the attribute values in this task are not uniformly distributed, particularly for gender, professional title and language. Assuming that the data distribution in the verification set is same as that in the training set, even if we do nothing but directly set the gender of all scholars as "male", the language as "Chinese", the title as "Professor", homepage as "NULL", and email as "NULL" we can get a considerable score according to the evaluation rules. The estimated score is:

$$(89.7 + 41.9 + 68.8 + 20.1 + 19.6)/5 = 48.2$$

We submitted the verification set results according to the above default values, and the measured score was 47.91, which was very close to the estimated value. On the one hand, it verifies our previous distribution hypothesis, and on the other hand, it also provides a reference benchmark for participants. Only when the score exceeds 47.91 on the validation set can the effectiveness of the method be explained.

4.2 Experiment Result

In order to verify the effectiveness of the proposed methods in detail, we tested them on the validation set. There are 1961 samples in the validation set, of which 33.7% (661 samples) resort to "semi-structured extraction" and 66.3% (1300 samples) resort to "unstructured extraction". The test results are shown in Table 4.

Table 4. Recognition accuracy of each attribute in the valid set

Attribute	Semi-structured extraction	Unstructured extraction	All
Gender	99.19%	93.36%	95.60%
Language	94.04%	79.19%	80.26%
Homepage	99.64%	32.88%	54.17%
Title	98.03%	81.83%	87.63%
Email	94.94%	38.01%	58.01%
Average	**96.71%**	**65.05%**	**75.78%**

We finally achieved 75.78% accuracy on the validation data set, and the average accuracy of "semi-structured extraction" is as high as 96.71%. Theoretically, the accuracy of this part can reach 100%, but a small number of errors may be caused by manual labelling, page loading, program implementation and so on. It should be noted that the attribute value of "email" is obtained by recognizing the characters in the picture, and its accuracy also reaches 94.94%, which shows that the OCR method previously proposed is very effective.

The average accuracy of "unstructured extraction" is 65.05%, and the major loss point lies in the attributes of homepage and email. We can select scholars' homepages from Google search results (no more than 20 pages), but according to statistics, only about 40% of scholars' homepages are included in the search results. Similar situation also exists in the email attribute: a considerable proportion of scholars' email is not included in the relevant search pages. Within the limited search range, the accuracy of the above two attributes (30–40%) is still acceptable. In contrast, the extraction of the other three attributes (gender, language and professional title) can be completely transformed into text classification, and all of them have achieved high accuracy (round 80%).

5 Conclusion

Using the information extraction methods based on multi-strategies integration, we finally got the first place in the evaluation task of *CCKS*-2021 "Aminer scholar profiling". The test data are divided by features into two parts: one adopts "semi-structured extraction" and the other adopts "unstructured extraction". This strategy improves the final accuracy by at least 10% points. In order to extract the email attribute values embedded in the pictures, a special OCR scheme is designed, which can greatly improve the single item accuracy. In the unstructured extraction part, the statistical method is used for the attributes with obvious characteristics (gender and email), and the deep learning method is used for other attributes (title, language and homepage). The "Bert + Softmax" classification model is finally used in the actual development. Of course, we also have tried other variant deep learning models, but the result is not very different. When deep learning develops to a relatively mature stage on some specific tasks, it is more effective to focus on the specific character of the business and the pre-processing of the data.

References

1. Roh, Y., Heo, G., Whang, S.E.: A survey on data collection for machine learning: a big data - AI integration perspective. IEEE Trans. Knowl. Data Eng. 33(4), 1328–1347 (2021)
2. CCKS 2021: AMiner Scholar Profiling – Biendata. https://www.biendata.xyz/competition/ccks_aminer_profiling/. Accessed 6 Sept 2021
3. Evaluation Tasks of CCKS 2021. http://sigkg.cn/ccks2021/?page_id=27. Accessed 6 Sept 2021
4. Li, Q., et al.: A survey on text classification: from shallow to deep learning. arXiv:2008.00364 (2020)
5. Maron, M.E.: Automatic indexing: an experimental inquiry. J. ACM 8(3), 404–417 (1961)
6. Cover, T.M., Hart, P.E.: Nearest neighbor pattern classification. IEEE Trans. Inf. Theory 13(1), 21–27 (1967)
7. Joachims, T.: Text categorization with support vector machines: learning with many relevant features. In: Nédellec, C., Rouveirol, C. (eds.) ECML 1998. LNCS, vol. 1398, pp. 137–142. Springer, Heidelberg (1998). https://doi.org/10.1007/BFb0026683
8. Tai, K.S., Socher, R., Manning, C.D.: Improved semantic representations from tree-structured long short-term memory networks. In: Proceedings of the ACL 2015, pp. 1556–1566 (2015)
9. Liu, P., Qiu, X., Chen, X., Wu, S., Huang, X.: Multi-time scale long short-term memory neural network for modelling sentences and documents. In: Proceedings of the EMNLP 2015, pp. 2326–2335 (2015)
10. Kim, Y.: Convolutional neural networks for sentence classification. In: Proceedings of the EMNLP 2014, pp. 1746–1751 (2014)
11. Shimura, K., Li, J., Fukumoto, F.: HFT-CNN: learning hierarchical category structure for multi-label short text categorization. In: Proceedings of the EMNLP 2018, pp. 811–816 (2018)
12. Peng, H., et al.: Large-scale hierarchical text classification with recursively regularized deep graph-CNN. In: Proceedings of the WWW 2018, pp. 1063–1072 (2018)
13. Yao, L., Mao, C., Luo, Y.: Graph convolutional networks for text classification. In: Proceedings of the AAAI 2019, pp. 7370–7377 (2019)
14. Devlin, J., Chang, M., Lee, K., Toutanova, K.: BERT: pre-training of deep bidirectional transformers for language understanding. In: Proceedings of the NAACL 2019, pp. 4171–4186 (2019)
15. Yang, Z., Dai, Z., Yang, Y., Carbonell, J.G., Salakhutdinov, R., Le, Q.V.: XLNet: generalized autoregressive pretraining for language understanding. In: Proceedings of the NeurIPS 2019, pp. 5754–5764 (2019)

Named Entity Recognition and Event Extraction in Chinese Electronic Medical Records

Cheng Ma[1] and Wenkang Huang[2(⊠)]

[1] Fudan University, Shanghai, China
19210240239@fudan.edu.cn
[2] Ant Group, Hangzhou, China
wenkang.hwk@alibaba-inc.com

Abstract. The China Conference on Knowledge Graph and Semantic Computing (CCKS) 2021 Evaluation Task 4 presented clinical named entity recognition and event extraction for the Chinese electronic medical records. Two annotated data sets for the two subtasks were provided for participators. Our model on the test dataset achieves the strict F1-Measure of 0.7684 which ranked the first place.

Keywords: CCKS · Named entity recognition · Event extraction

1 Introduction

With the advent of the information age, electronic medical records have become more and more popular. Electronic medical records contain a large amount of medical semantic knowledge. It is particularly important to use effective natural language processing technology to extract the knowledge contained in electronic medical records. CCKS 2021 sets up five evaluation themes and a total of fourteen evaluation tasks, task 4 focuses on named entity recognition (NER) and event extraction (EE) in the Chinese electronic medical records (EMR).

NER and EE are commonly used techniques to extract structured knowledge from unstructured text. The most popular NER method is sequence labeling, which can be based on long short-term memory (LSTM) [1,2] or bidirectional encoder representation from transformers (BERT) [3]. Sometimes, medical event extraction can be transformed into a medical entity recognition task.

In this paper, we use the medical named entity recognition data set and medical event extraction data set provided by CCKS 2021 task 4. By using the pre-trained BERT model and fusing multiple models based on the expansion of the BERT model, we obtained a strict F1 score of 0.7684 based on the data set provided by CCKS 2021 Task 4.

© Springer Nature Singapore Pte Ltd. 2022
B. Qin et al. (Eds.): CCKS 2021, CCIS 1553, pp. 133–138, 2022.
https://doi.org/10.1007/978-981-19-0713-5_15

2   Task Formalism

2.1   Clinical Named Entity Recognition (CNER)

This task is a Chinese medical record medical entity recognition task, that is, for a given set of plain text documents of electronic medical records, identify and extract entity mentions related to medical clinics, and classify them into pre-defined categories, such as disease, drug, operation, etc.

Formalized Definition. We define this task formally.
INPUT:

1) A document collection from EMR: $D = \{d_1, d_2, ..., d_N\}$, where $d_i = (w_{i1}, ..., w_{in})$
2) A set of pre-defined categories: $C = \{c_1, ..., c_m\}$.

OUTPUT:
Collections of entity mention-category pairs: $\{(m_1, c_{m1}), ..., (m_i, c_{mi}), (m_p, c_{mp})\}$.

The $m_i = (d_i, b_i, e_i)$ represent the entity mention in document d_i, where b_i and e_i is the start and end position of m_i, respectively. $c_{mi} \in C$ represents the category of m_i. The overlap between mentions is not allowed, which is $e_i < b_{i+1}$.

Pre-defined Categories. There are 6 categories that are defined as follows.

1) Disease and diagnose (Dis)
2) Imaging examination (ImgExam)
3) Laboratory examination (LabExam)
4) Operation
5) Drug
6) Anatomy

2.2   Clinical Event Extraction (CEE)

This task is the task of extracting medical events from Chinese medical records, that is, given the main entity of the electronic medical record text data of the tumor, define several attributes of the tumor event, such as tumor size, tumor primary site, etc., identify and extract events and attributes, and perform text structure change.

Formalized Definition. This task is formally defined as follows.
INPUT:

1) Event entity.
2) A document collection from EMR: $D = d_1, ..., d_N$, where $d_i = (w_{i1}, ..., w_{in})$
3) A set of pre-defined attributes: $P = p_1, p_2, ..., p_m$

OUTPUT:
Collections of attribute entities: $\{[d_i, (p_j, (s_1, s_2, ..., s_k))]\}$, and $1 \leq i \leq N, 1 \leq j \leq m$. The s_k is the entity of attribute p_j from document d_i. There could be 0 or more than one entity for each attribute.

Pre-defined Categories. The 3 pre-defined attributes are:

1) Tumor Primary Site
2) Tumor Size
3) Tumor Metastatic Site

3   Methods

3.1   BERT Encoder

Bidirectional encoder representation from transformers (BERT) is a pre-trained language mode based on a large-scale universal corpus, which has two self-supervision task, next sentence prediction and masked language model. BERT learns a large amount of general knowledge through the task of self-supervision, and it only needs simple fine-tuning to transfer the knowledge to downstream tasks, so as to get better results.

3.2   Conditional Random Fields (CRF)

A conditional random field (CRF) is a type of discriminative, undirected probabilis tic graphical model, which has been widely used for sequence labeling problems. For a given character sequence $z = z_1, ..., z_n$, where z_n is the input vector composed of the char and features of ith character, and a given label sequence $y = y_1, ..., y_n$ for z. $\gamma(z)$ represent the all of possible labels for z. The CRF model define the formula of the probability of character sequence y with given label sequence y is:

$$p(y|z; \theta) = \frac{\sum_{t=1}^{n} exp(S(y^{(t)}, z^{(t)}, \theta))}{\sum_{t=1}^{n} \sum_{j \in \gamma(z)} exp(S(y_j, z^{(t)}, \theta))} \tag{1}$$

Where $S(y^{(t)}, z^{(t)}, \theta)$ are potential function, and θ is the parameters of CRF. In our work, we use the character as a unit for sequence labeling model rather than use the word. Log likelihood function was used to get the loss of the CRF layer. Finally, the viterbi algorithm was used to decode.

3.3   Transform of Event Extraction

In the event extraction task, we need to identify the three positions of the tumor primary site, tumor metastasis site, and tumor size in a piece of text. We convert these three positions into entity type tags, and then turn this task into entity Identify the task.

Because the original data only gives the characters of the tumor primary site, tumor metastasis site, and tumor size, but not the position in the text. When transforming the event extraction task into an entity recognition task, we need to mark the location of the tumor primary site, tumor metastasis site, and tumor size in the text.

We noticed that the word "转移" (transfer) appears in many texts, which is very important for the identification of the metastasis site. Therefore, for the confirmation of the physical location of the metastasis site, the method we choose is to select the entity location closest to the word "转移".

4 Evalution Metrics

4.1 Clinical Named Entity Recognition

This task uses Precision, Recall and F1-Measure as evaluation metrics. The extracted entities set is denoted as $S = s_1, s_2, ..., s_m$ and the gold entities set is denoted as $G = g_1, g_2, ..., g_n$. The set element is an entity mention, expressed as a four-tuple $<d, pos_b, pos_e, c>$; where d represents a document, pos_b and pos_e respectively correspond to the start and end of the entity mention in document d, c indicates that the entity mentions the predefined category to which it belongs. There are two evaluation metrics, the strict metric and relaxed metric.

Strict Metric. For the strict metric, $s_i \in S$ is equal to $g_j \in G$, which means they are exactly the same:

1) $s_i[d] = g_j[d]$
2) $s_i[pos_b] = g_j[pos_b]$
3) $s_i[pos_e] = g_j[pos_e]$
4) $s_i[c] = g_j[c]$.

The strict Precision, Recall and F1 can be calculated as follows:

$$P_s = \frac{|S \cap_s G|}{|S|} \tag{2}$$

$$R_s = \frac{|S \cap_s G|}{|G|} \tag{3}$$

$$F1_s = \frac{2P_s R_s}{P_s + R_s} \tag{4}$$

Relaxed Metric. The relaxed metric does not require that $s_i \in S$ and $g_j \in G$ are exactly the same, and they only need to meet the following requirements:

1) $s_i[d] = g_j[d]$
2) $max(s_i[pos_b], g_j[pos_b]) \leq min(s_i[pos_e], g_j[pos_e])$
3) $s_i[c] = g_j[c]$.

The relaxed Precision, Recall and F1 can be calculated as follows:

$$P_r = \frac{|S \cap_r G|}{|S|} \tag{5}$$

$$R_r = \frac{|S \cap_r G|}{|G|} \tag{6}$$

$$F1_r = \frac{2P_r R_r}{P_r + R_r} \tag{7}$$

4.2 Clinical Event Extraction

There could be more than one attribute entity for an event attribute. The Precision, Recall and F1 are calculated based on the attribute entity rather then attribute.

5 Experiments

5.1 Datasets

The CCKS 2021 Task 4 provided annotated data set for Clinical Named Entity Recognition and Clinical Event Extraction. The statistics of CNER and CEE data set are shown in Table 1 and Table 2 respectively.

Table 1. The statistics of clinical named entity recognition data set.

	Docs	Dis	ImgExam	LabExam	Operation	Drug	Anatonmy	Total
Train	1050	4345	1002	1297	923	1935	8811	18313
Valid	450	1834	481	575	406	894	3861	8051
Unlabeled	1000	–	–	–	–	–	–	–

Table 2. The statistics of clinical event extraction data set.

	Docs	TumorPrimarySite	TumorSize	TumorMetastaticSite	Total
Train	1000	1075	1025	1878	3978
Valid	400	269	260	638	1167
Unlabeled	1000	–	–	–	–

5.2 Settings

By adjusting the hyper-parameters of the training model through the validation datasets, the best hyper-parameters in CRF model was obtained and described below. The model are trained by Adam optimization algorithm [4].

1) Learning-rate of CRF layer is 5e-5.
2) Learning-rete of BERT layer is 2e-5.

We also used adversarial training (such as FGM [5]) and other tricks to improve the model results.

5.3   Results

The results of our model on the validation set are shown in the Table 3 and Table 4 respectively. Compared strict and relaxed results in Table 3, we find that the operations don't have a high strict F-measure but have a high relaxed F-measure. It means that the right position of entities has been found without the right boundary. It can be seen from Table 4 that the model does not recognize the primary site of the tumor very well, possibly because the word "转移" does not provide enough information for the recognition of the primary site.

Table 3. The results of clinical named entity recognition on Valid data sets.

	Dis	ImgExam	LabExam	Operation	Drug	Anatonmy	All
Strict	0.870	0.893	0.884	0.876	0.942	0.868	0.880
Relaxed	0.943	0.935	0.935	0.950	0.970	0.940	0.944

Table 4. The statistics of clinical event extraction on Valid data set.

	TumorPrimarySite	TumorSize	TumorMetastaticSite	All
Strict	0.736	0.912	0.814	0.800

6   Conclusion

This paper presents a detailed introduction of CCKS 2021 Task4 for clinical named entity recognition and clinical event extraction for Chinese EMRs. Our team won the first place in the Task 4 evaluation with a combined score of 0.7684. We will focus on the more effective extraction of entities' boundary in the future.

References

1. Lample, G., et al.: Neural architectures for named entity recognition. In: Proceedings of the 2016 Conference of the North American Chapter of the Association for Computational Linguistics: Human Language Technologies, pp. 260–270 (2016)
2. Ma, X.Z., Hovy, E.: End-to-end sequence labeling via bi-directional LSTM-CNNs-CRF. In: Proceedings of the 54th Annual Meeting of the Association for Computational Linguistics, pp. 1064–1074 (2016)
3. Devlin, J., et al.: BERT: pre-training of deep bidirectional transformers for language understanding. arXiv preprint arXiv:1810.04805 (2018)
4. Kingma, D.P., Ba, J.: Adam: a method for stochastic optimization. arXiv preprint arXiv:1412.6980 (2014)
5. Miyato, T., Dai, A.M., Goodfellow, I.: Adversarial Training Methods for Semi-Supervised Text Classification. arXiv preprint arXiv:1605.07725 (2017)

Strategies for Enhancing Generalization Ability of Communication Event Co-reference Resolution

Xi Yu[✉], Xuehan Bai[✉], Shukai Liao, and Hongyan Cui

Beijing University of Posts and Telecommunications:, Beijing, China
baixuehan@bupt.edu.cn

Abstract. There are many different expressions for the same event. The goal of event co-reference resolution is to build a calculation model for the similarity of event expressions to achieve the unity of data. Based on the Roberta pre-trained model, aiming at the problem of unbalanced distribution of difficult and easy cases in data, the effectiveness of various methods to enhance the generalization ability of the model is explored, including different data input methods, data enhancement, different loss functions, adversarial learning, contrastive learning. The best data input and model training methods are finally selected. On the CCKS2021 event co-reference resolution task for communication field, the f1 value of single model reaches 0.80 in test dataset 1 and 0.89 in test dataset 2.

Keywords: Event co-reference resolution · Generalization · Contrastive learning · Data enhancement

Mathematics Subject Classification (2020): 68T50 · 68U15

1 Introduction

Event co-reference resolution is a subtask of event extraction. It was first proposed by Ahn [1] when studying event extraction. Event extraction needs to identify event trigger (Trigger) and event type (Type), and extract event element (Argument) and determine its role (Argument Role). Therefore, the accuracy of event extraction is one of the most important factors that determine the difficulty of event co-reference resolution. Compared with event co-reference resolution, the current research on entity co-reference is more mature. Entity co-reference resolution usually uses statistical features (prior probability, edit distance, boolean features, Jacobi similarity, etc.), semantic features (based on Word2vec, pre-trained language model, word semantic clustering, etc.), graph (random walk, etc.) to calculate entity similarity. Since event co-reference resolution involves more sentence elements and the expression of the same event is more abundant, it is necessary to consider the similarity of trigger and event elements and the overall expression, and integrate a large number of domain knowledge and linguistic knowledge. At present, the common event co-reference

© Springer Nature Singapore Pte Ltd. 2022
B. Qin et al. (Eds.): CCKS 2021, CCIS 1553, pp. 139–150, 2022.
https://doi.org/10.1007/978-981-19-0713-5_16

resolution method is to calculate the similarity scores of event description statement and each pair of attributes [2].

In this paper, event co-reference resolution is carried out for Fault Handling Process Knowledge in communication field. In the process of communication operation and maintenance, the knowledge of Fault Handling Process is analyzed through 'event' and 'event relationship', providing troubleshooting and failure recovery solutions, and guiding the frontline to deal with existing network failures. As shown in Fig. 1. The task is defined as follows: Given text T1, T2, event e1 in T1 and event e2 in T2, determine whether e1 and e2 are equal.

e1: {"text": "PTN 链上端站交叉板隐性问题导致部分 TDS 站点下 PS 掉线率指标恶化及交互类业务异常问题", "trigger": ["IndexFault", 31, "恶化"], "argument": [["Index", 18, "TDS 站点下 PS 掉线率指标"]]},

e2: {"text": "PS 掉线率升高的问题", "trigger": ["IndexFault", 5, "升高"], "argument": [["Index", 0, "PS 掉线率"]]}

Fig. 1. Cases of e1 and e2

According to the types of trigger, all the data can be divided into eight categories: IndexFault, SoftHardwareFault, CollectData, Check, SettingFault, ExternalFault, SetMachine, and Operate. Different types of events have different event elements. Different from the common event co-reference resolution, this task has the following difficulties:

1. Field characteristics are obvious and there are many terminology.
2. There are missing extraction and missing text description.
3. Unbalanced distribution of cases.

Due to the above difficulties, the generalization performance of the basic model is weak. Based on these problems, the main contributions of this paper are:

1. Aiming at the obvious problem of domain features, fine-tuning is performed on the large-scale pre-trained language model Roberta.
2. Aiming at the problem of missing event extraction and text description, a variety of data input methods are tried, including using only event statements, combining overall description with event statements, and integrating trigger words with event element names.
3. To solve the problem of uneven distribution of difficult and easy cases, data enhancement, different loss functions, adversarial learning, contrastive learning, joint global and local models are explored.
4. The effect of different methods is verified by experiments, and the best data input and model training methods are finally selected to enhance the generalization ability of Roberta event co-reference model in the field of communication.

2   Related Work

There has been a lot of work to deal with event co-reference tasks by machine learning. Chen [3] jointly infers different syntactic types by training multiple classifiers. Lee [4], Liu [5] and others improved the effect of event coreference resolution by introducing knowledge bases such as WordNet and FrameNet. Zeng [6] introduced convolutional neural network into entity relation classification task for the first time, reflecting the effectiveness of deep learning in relation classification task. Krause [7], Santos [8] improved the effect of homonym resolution to some extent by considering the position information between words in the neural network. Fang Jie [9] proposed CorefNet, a convolutional neural network model with multi-attention mechanism, which mainly solves the problem that event features are difficult to obtain. By using the attention mechanism, filter important features, and determine whether the two events refer to the same by fusing the features of two events. Hu Min [10] proposed a method based on multi-head attention mechanism to judge event coreference, and different attention can capture different features.

The above methods include a variety of solutions to event resolution, but traditional machine learning methods strongly rely on artificial feature, while the introduction of external knowledge such as WordNet lacks stability. Although the event resolution method based on deep learning can automatically extract features, the method based on convolutional neural network cannot effectively pay attention to the semantic order in the event description text and lack the consideration of location characteristics.

Generalization ability refers to the ability of the algorithm to adapt to fresh new samples, that is, whether the model can draw inferences from one another. The model with good generalization ability can learn the rules hidden behind the training set data, and give the appropriate output for the data outside the learning set with the same rule. Adjusting the training data or abstracting the problem definition may greatly improve the generalization. The main methods include obtaining more training data, transforming the data, adding noise, data enhancement, feature selection, etc. The generalization performance can also be improved by tuning the algorithm, mainly including regularization, adjusting the activation function, learning rate, network structure and so on. In addition, merging multiple models can also improve performance. The greater the difference between models, the better the effect. In recent years, more and more studies have found that multitasking learning can also improve the generalization ability of the model. Multiple tasks share parameters, and more features can be learned to a certain extent. This paper will explore different schemes to improve generalization performance, and finally choose the best data input and model training method.

3   Model Introduction

3.1   Event Co-reference Framework

Figure 2 shows the overall model architecture diagram. The pre-trained language model Roberta is used to process text to obtain semantic information. Then the sentence embedding is passed through a simple multi-layer perceptron classifier. The model judges similar event pairs as True examples, and different event pairs as False classes, and uses Focal loss as the loss function to train a two-class model.

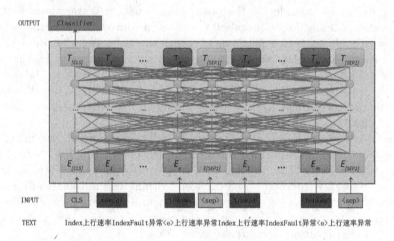

Fig. 2. Event co-reference model diagram based on Roberta

3.2   Generalization Ability Enhancement Strategy

The experiment found that due to the difference of the data, the accuracy rate on the test data set 1 and the test data set 2 is far lower than the training set. At the same time, the classification probability is statistically distributed, and it is found that most of the probabilities are distributed in the interval of 0–0.1, 0.9–1. It shows that most events are very similar or dissimilar, and there are few difficult cases. This may be one of the main reasons for the low generalization performance of the model.

We adopt a generalization enhancement strategy including data enhancement, different loss functions, adversarial learning, comparative learning, and joint global and local model.

In addition, in order to effectively combine the location information of events and consider the relationship between event elements, this paper attempts to combine event attribute name and event content in a variety of ways. It includes offset, semantics and order. The offset method refers to the order of occurrence in the original text. This method restores the order of the original text as much as possible. According to semantics refers to the fixed syntactic components, which conforms to the semantic order of Chinese. Order refers to the order of data given, which brings the most noise.

The following describes how different strategies are applied in the model.

3.2.1   Data Enhancement

Data enhancement is the simplest method to enhance the generalization ability of the model. Data enhancement can be used to increase the amount of training data and increase the noise data to improve the robustness of the model. The image can be enhanced by rotating, flipping, cropping, blurring and other methods. However, due to the particularity of the language, it is difficult to guarantee that the semantics will not change after the language is transformed. We considered the explicit and implicit embedding layer for data enhancement method.

1. EDA (Easy Data Augmentation) data enhancement
   In the process of the experiment, it was found that the precision is low, and the cases judged as True actually contain a large amount of False data, indicating that the model has a poor ability to judge False examples. Therefore, we consider enhancing the False examples in the training set. Trigger words in False cases are replaced with Synonyms Replace, Randomly Insert, and Randomly Delete.
   (a) Synonym replacement: randomly select a word and replace it with synonyms;
   (b) Random insertion: randomly select a word and insert synonyms;
   (c) Random deletion: each word in the sentence is deleted randomly with probability p = 0.1.
2. Token shuffling
   Token shuffling refers to shuffling the order of data input with a certain probability. Transfomer obtains the order of input data through position embedding, so it can be shuffled directly
3. Adversarial learning
   Increase interference through adversarial learning. FGM (Fast Gradient Method) is to add noise to the embedding parameter matrix to increase the gradient.

3.2.2   Loss Function

We regard event co-reference as a classification model. For classification models, cross-entropy loss function is generally used to measure the similarity between two probability distributions. During the experiment, the simple cases in the training set are far greater than the difficult cases. The easy-to-classify cases account for most of the loss, which obscures the importance of the difficult cases. Therefore, we use Focal loss to balance the importance of difficult and easy samples.

3.2.3   Contrastive Learning

Multi-task learning is a means to improve the generalization performance of the model. It uses the internal relationship between tasks to improve the generalization performance of single task learning. Therefore, we verified the experimental effect of adding contrastive learning. Contrastive learning is to zoom in on similar data and isolate dissimilar data on the hyperplane, which is divided into supervised and unsupervised way. In this paper, we use self-supervised contrastive learning.

As shown in Fig. 3, the specific method is that the training data is first back-translated, and then the data of textA and textB are converted. The data after back-translated and converted form a similar sample with the original data, and the original data form a different sample with other data in the training set. Considering the different tasks of CLS in different layers of the pre-trained language model, the CLS output in the tenth layer of the model is better for contrastive learning. The overall model is as follows:

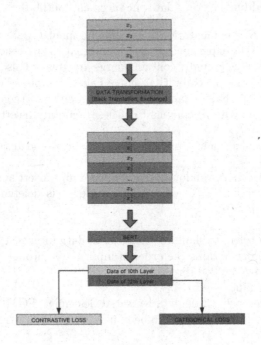

Fig. 3. Multi-task learning model

The loss function of self-supervised contrastive learning is shown in formula 1

$$li, j = -log \frac{exp(sim(zi, zj)/\tau)}{\sum_{k=1}^{2N} \mathbb{1}_{[k \neq i]} exp(sim(zi, zj)/\tau)} \tag{1}$$

3.2.4 Joint Global and Local Model

For process events in the communication field, the event is composed of trigger words and event elements. The co-referential events must satisfy the consistency of trigger words, the same elements of the event, and the consistency of the event as a whole. Based on the above conditions, we propose a joint global and local model, that is, to compare whether the above three are co-referential, as shown in Fig. 4

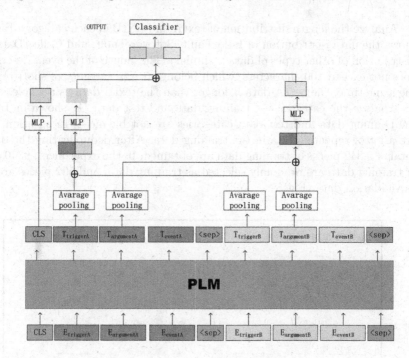

Fig. 4. Global and local joint model

The input data format is:

text_a =line['eventA']['trigger'][2] + ' ' +'<b>' + line['eventA']['argument'][1][2] + ' ' + line['eventA']['argument'][0][2] + ' ' + line['eventA']['argument'][1][2] + '<e>' + line['eventA']['argument'][1][2] + line['eventA']['argument'][0][2] + line['eventA']['trigger'][2] + line['eventA']['argument'][1][2] + '<texta_e>'

The data format of text_b and text_a is the same.

<b>, <e>, and <texta_e> are three identifiers respectively. The text_a, text_b trigger words and event element vectors are averaged as their expressions. Then, the trigger words and event element vectors of text_a and text_b are combined, and the similarity is classified and judged through the MLP (multilayer perceptron) layer. CLS is still used as the overall similarity vector. The three similarities are merged through the linear layer, and the most appropriate weights are fitted to each part to jointly judge co-reference.

4   Experiment

4.1   Data Analysis and Processing

For Fault Handling Process Knowledge in communication field, the training set has 15,000 data, the first test data set has 2,000 data, and the second test data set has 29,000 data, of which 2,000 are real test data and the others are interference data.

Analyze the length distribution of textA and textB in each category. Figure 4 shows the data distribution of IndexFault, SoftwareFault, and CollectData (the distribution of other types of data is similar). The length of the event description does not exceed 100 characters, which belongs to the category of short text. At the same time, the textA data is longer than the textB data as a whole.

Analyze the categories of training data and test data. As shown in Table 1, the training data and test data categories are not balanced. In addition, there are a lot of repeated data in the training data. After deduplicating the data, a total of 9,842 pieces of training data are obtained. In the experiment, 9340 pieces of training data are randomly selected as training data, and 502 pieces are used as validation data (Fig. 5).

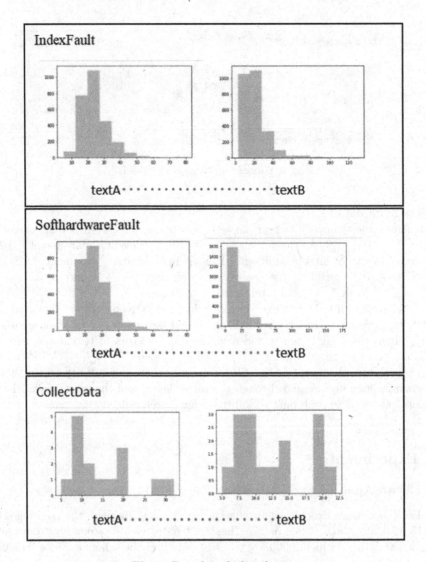

Fig. 5. Data length distribution

Table 1. Train and test data category distribution

Category	Train	Test1
IndexFault	3192	745
SoftHardwareFault	6597	861
CollectData	15	0
Check	770	31
SettingFault	1871	125
ExternalFault	0	0
SetMachine	1228	115
Operate	1327	123

4.2 Analysis of Experimental Results

1. Result analysis of test data set 1.
   Since there is a lot of noise that is not related to the event in the overall sentence, we only use the extracted event description in the subsequent experiments. As shown in Table 2, the trigger and event elements are spliced in semantic order to compare the effects of different loss functions and adversarial learning. Id = 1, the Ernie model is used as the baseline, and the loss function uses cross-entropy loss. At this time, f1 can reach 0.774, but the precision is significantly lower than recall, indicating that the data that the model judges to be True contains a large number of False examples. Id = 2, using Focal loss, precision increased by 0.02, and recall decreased. Id = 3, add adversarial learning on the basis of id = 2. The recall and f1 values are improved while keeping the accuracy. It indicates that the simultaneous use of Focal loss and confrontational learning can improve the generalization of the model.

Table 2. Results of different loss functions and adversarial learning

Id	Model	Data input	p	r	f1
1	Ernie crossentropy loss	Semantic	0.68	0.89	0.7740
2	Ernie focalloss	Semantic	0.70	0.87	0.778
3	Ernie focalloss FGM	Semantic	0.70	0.88	0.7833

Table 3 shows the experimental results obtained by data enhancement or changing the data input mode on the optimal model in Table 2. Id = 4, compared with id = 3, only EDA is performed on the data, and the precision is significantly improved, indicating that the discrimination ability of the model for False cases is enhanced. However, recall also decreased significantly and the overall f1 value increased slightly, indicating that EDA can effectively turn the easily classified cases in the False cases into difficult cases during training. Id = 5, connect trigger words and event elements according to offset. At this time, compared with id = 3, f1 decreases significantly. It is speculated that the data is too standardized and the rules learned by the model are relatively simple, so the generalization performance decreases. Id = 6, connect according to offset and apply EDA at the same time. The increase of f1 value indicates that adding disturbance to the data is conducive to the generalization performance. Id = 7, first, trigger and event elements are connected with attribute names, and then the data is connected in semantic order. Compared with id = 1, the effect of adding attribute names is only slightly improved; Id = 8, also add the attribute name. Compared with id = 5, adding the attribute name provides more information and has a certain improvement; Id = 8, also add the attribute name. Compared with id = 5, adding the attribute name provides more information and has a certain improvement; Id = 9, on the basis of 8, plus token shuffling, basically no improvement. Id = 10, using a five-fold cross-training method for training on a model, f1 reaches 0.795, indicating that the cross-training has learned more features and the generalization performance is better. Id = 11, change the pre-trained language model to Roberta, and f1 reaches 0.8, indicating that the Roberta model is more effective than Ernie for this type of data event resolution.

Table 3. Result of data enhancement or change of data input method

Id	Model	Data input	p	r	f1
3	Ernie focalloss FGM	Semantic	0.70	0.88	0.7833
4	Ernie focalloss FGM	semanticEDA	0.78	0.84	0.78826
5	Ernie focalloss FGM	Offset	0.74	0.75	0.75
6	Ernie focalloss FGM	offsetEDA	0.75	0.825	0.787
7	Ernie focalloss FGM	Attribute name, semantic	0.69	0.88	0.7874
8	Ernie focalloss FGM	Attribute name, offset	0.72	0.87	0.78988
9	Ernie focalloss FGM	Attribute name, offset 0.1token shuffle	0.70	0.88	0.7815
10	Ernie focalloss FGM	Offset 5-fold	0.72	0.87	0.79551
11	Roberta focalloss FGM	Offset 5-fold	0.72	0.88	0.800

Table 4 shows the effect of using self-supervised contrastive learning. Because the last layer CLS of the pre-trained language model is generally used to judge the similarity of two sentences, if it is directly used in comparative learning, the effect will be very poor. In this experiment, we use the tenth layer CLS. However, on the whole, f1 decreased. Our analysis is because self-supervised contrastive learning requires a large amount of data. However, there are few experimental data. Similar samples are too similar, and the model learns fewer features, which reduces the f1 value of event co-reference resolution task.

Table 4. Effect of self-supervised contrastive learning

Model	Data input	p	r	f1
Self-supervised contrastive learning, Event co-reference	offset	0.69	0.82	0.75

Table 5 shows the results of global and local joint model, which have little effect.

Table 5. The results of global and local joint model

Model	Data input	p	r	f1
Global and local joint model	See 3.2.4 description	0.71	0.84	0.784

2. Result analysis of test data set 2

   Due to the large difference between test data set 1 and test data set 2, we find that the optimal model on test data set 1 has poor effect on test data set 2. Table 6 shows the results of different models on test data set 2. The optimal model is id = 2. Using Roberta, FGM and focalloss, the input number is offset with attribute name, and the F1 value reaches 0.8979. In addition, we also tried to translate the attribute name, which had little effect.

Table 6. Results of different models on test data set 2

Id	Model	Data input	p	r	f1
1	Roberta large FGM Focalloss	attribute name +<e>+offsett	0.8568	0.93775	0.8954
2	Roberta FGM Focalloss	attribute name +<e>+offset	0.86	0.938	0.8979
3	Roberta large FGM Focalloss	attribute name +<e>+offset 0.1 token shuffle	0.8769	0.9055	0.8929
4	Roberta large FGM Focalloss	Translate (attribute name) +<e>+offset	0.86	0.92	0.8932

5   Summary

This paper mainly focuses on the event co-reference for Fault Handling Process Knowledge in communication field. Aiming at the problem of uneven distribution of event knowledge data in the communication field, this paper explores a variety of methods to improve the generalization of the model, mainly including data enhancement, different loss functions, adversarial learning, contrastive learning, the combination of global and local models, and finally selects the best data input and model training method. On CCKS2021 event co-reference resolution task for communication field, the f1 value of single model reaches 0.80 in test data set 1 and 0.89 in test data set 2. Because the experimental results are limited by the effect of event extraction, many generalization methods do not play a great role. Therefore, we will continue to explore how to better integrate into the overall text for event co referential resolution.

References

1. Ahn, D.: The stages of event extraction. In: Proceedings of the Workshop of the ACL on Annotating and Reasoning about Time and Events, pp. 1–8 (2006)
2. Wang, J., Song, X., Du, H.: Research on synonymous expression pattern extraction for coreference event recognition. J. China Soc. Sci. Tech. Inf. **39**(03), 297–307 (2020)
3. Chen, B., Su, J., Pan, S.J., Tan, C.L.: A unified event coreference resolution by integrating multiple resolvers. In: Proceedings of the 5th International Joint Conference on Natural Language Processing, pp. 102–110 (2011)
4. Lee, H., Recasens, M., Chang, A., Surdeanu, M., Jurafsky, D.: Joint entity and event coreference resolution across documents. In: Proceedings of Empirical Methods in Natural Language Processing and Computational Natural Language Learning, pp. 489–500 (2012)
5. Liu, Z., Araki, J., Hovy, E., Mitamura, T.: Supervised within-document event coreference using information propagation. In: Proceedings of the Ninth International Conference on Language Resources and Evaluation, pp. 4539–4544 (2014)
6. Zeng, D., Liu, K., Lai, S., Zhou, G., Zhao, J.: Relation classification via convolutional deep neural network. In: COLING, pp. 2335–2344. The Association for Computational Linguistics (2014)
7. Krause, S., Xu, F., Uszkoreit, H., Weissenborn, D.: Event linking with sentential features from convolutional neural networks. In: Proceedings of the 20th SIGNLL Conference on Computational Natural Language Learning (CoNLL), pp. 239–249 (2016)
8. dos Santos, C.N., Xiang, B., Zhou, B.: Classifying relations by ranking with convolutional neural networks. In: ACL, vol. 1, pp. 626–634. The Association for Computational Linguistic (2015)
9. Jie, F., Li, P., Zhu, Q.: An event reference resolution method based on multi-attention mechanism. Comput. Sci. **46**(8), 277–281 (2019)
10. Eunmin, C.H., Peifeng, L.: Chinese event coreference resolution method based on structured representation. J. Chin. Inf. Process. **33**(12), 19–27 (2019)

Unmanned Aerial Vehicle Knowledge Graph Construction with SpERT

Yike Wu, Yipeng Zhu, Jingchen Li, Chengye Zhang, Tianling Gong, Xiyuan Du, and Tianxing Wu[✉]

School of Computer Science and Engineering, Southeast University, Nanjing, China
tianxingwu@seu.edu.cn

Abstract. Unmanned aerial vehicles are becoming more and more important in the military field. In recent years, global hot spot military events and local conflicts have fully proved its military value. Since knowledge graph is the information basis of intelligence, how to build a high-quality unmanned aerial vehicle knowledge graph is the focus of this paper. In this work, we propose an effective method to construct a knowledge graph from textual data. We first build the schema manually based on our domain knowledge. We then extract RDF triples with SpERT. Third, we disambiguate the instance by string comparison. Finally, We import the knowledge graph into neo4j for visualization. Our team takes part in the No. 10 evaluation task (i.e., military domain-specific knowledge graph construction for military unmanned aerial vehicles) in CCKS 2021. There are two stages in this evaluation, and our approach achieves the second place in the first stage, i.e., knowledge graph quality evaluation and the third place in the second stage, i.e., knowledge graph usage evaluation.

Keywords: SpERT · Unmanned aerial vehicle · Knowledge graph

1 Introduction

Unmanned aerial vehicles occupy an increasingly important position in the military competition of various countries. They have become an indispensable part of modern wars. Thus, studying unmanned aerial vehicles relevant techniques is of great significance to armament development. A knowledge graph in this area can greatly promote the development of intelligent techniques on unmanned aerial vehicles. However, there is no mature knowledge graph. Therefore, a high-quality knowledge graph is definitely necessary.

Nowadays, knowledge graph has become more and more important as an AI technology in daily life. Compared with traditional relational database, it is more convenient for people to search information and easier to expand and update. Thus, an unmanned aerial vehicle knowledge graph can not only provide a large number of information, but also support downstream applications, such as question answering and man-machine conversation. Besides, a high-quality

© Springer Nature Singapore Pte Ltd. 2022
B. Qin et al. (Eds.): CCKS 2021, CCIS 1553, pp. 151–159, 2022.
https://doi.org/10.1007/978-981-19-0713-5_17

knowledge graph is beneficial to the research, providing essential information to help develop the next generation of unmanned aerial vehicles. However, how to construct knowledge graph effectively in this area is a difficult problem, so it is meaningful to explore effective methods to finish the building task.

In this paper, we construct a unmanned aerial vehicle knowledge graph from textual data using SpERT (Span-based Entity and Relation Transformer) [2]. The construction process is mainly divided into four steps: schema construction, information extraction, instance disambiguation, and knowledge graph visualization.

2   Related Work

Construction Methods for Knowledge Graph. There are two ways on knowledge graph construction, i.e., top-down construction and bottom-up construction [3]. The top-down construction method refers to determining the schema of the knowledge graph at first, and then filling in instance data to form the knowledge graph. The bottom-up construction method refers to collecting instance data in the form of triples at first, and then building the schema based on the data content. Given that we plan to build a knowledge graph on a specific domain and the schema is relatively easy to define, we choose the top-down method.

Methods for Information Extraction. For information extraction, due to the limitation of the evaluation task, we could only use the given textual data to get instances and their properties, which means we have to build the knowledge graph from unstructured data. There are three main approaches. The first is based on rules and patterns. The second is applying statistical models. The last one is extracting information employing deep learning models. The rules and patterns in the given textual data are not obvious and the statistical models rely on complex feature engineering, so we focus on the third method. The third method can also be divided into two types. One is pipeline models, and the other is joint extraction models. Pipeline models first extract instances and their relations while joint extraction models extract both at the same time. Pipeline models are prone to the propagation of errors from instance extraction, so there is a line of research joint extraction models [6] which can overcome the weak points of pipeline models. Miwa and Sasaki [5] model this problem as table-filling problems. Miwa and Bansal [4] exploit traditional neural network models, LSTM and RNN to tackle this problem. Markus Eberts and Adrian Ulges [2] propose SpERT to extract instances and their relations. In our work, considering the awesome performance of SpERT, we choose it to information extraction.

3   Knowledge Graph Construction

There are four steps in unmanned aerial vehicle knowledge graph construction, including schema construction, information extraction, instance disambiguation,

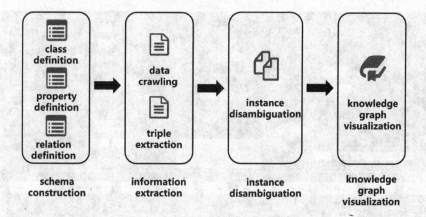

Fig. 1. The process of the knowledge graph construction.

and knowledge graph visualization. Neo4j is chosen as a platform to visualize the knowledge graph. The whole process is shown in Fig. 1.

3.1 Schema Construction

We construct the schema manually. In detail, we look up the relevant information of each specific class in the corpus published by CCKS 2021 evaluation track, and we try to find the potential class properties and the relations between classes. For example, for class *"unmanned aerial vehicle"*, the contextual text always describes the companies producing a specific kind of unmanned aerial vehicles and relevant equipments. Thus, we add classes *"company"* and *"equipment"*. Finally, as shown in Fig. 2, we design ten classes including *"unmanned aerial vehicle"*, *"equipment"*, *"location"*, *"facility"*, *"institution"*, *"people"*, *"war"*, *"troop"*, *"company"* and *"country"*. Besides, for each class, we design different properties, such as properties *"name"*, *"participating countries"*, *"result"* and *"location"* for the class *"war"*, and we have 31 properties in total. The relations between classes are also important elements in our schema (see Fig. 2), such as the relation *"participate in"* between *"unmanned aerial vehicle"* and *"war"*, and the relation *"manufacture"* between *"company"* and *"unmanned aerial vehicle"*.

3.2 Information Extraction

Information extraction consists of three steps: 1) we first crawl web text about unmanned aerial vehicles as an important complement of the corpus provided by the evaluation task; 2) we then apply the SpERT model [2] to extract RDF triples from textual data; 3) we finally integrate the same instances with different names by instance disambiguation.

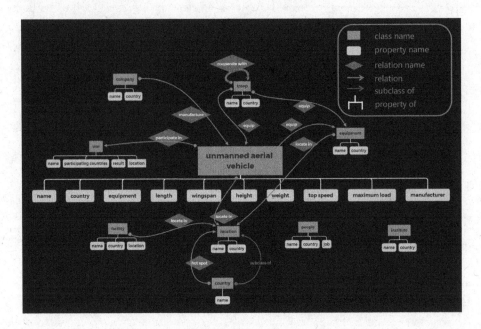

Fig. 2. The schema of our built knowledge graph.

Corpus. The basic corpus is published by CCKS 2021 evaluation task, which contains sixty documents. The evaluation task restricts that the extracted instances and relations should occur in the given corpus, but participants can add more training documents to better support extracting instances and their relations. Based on this, we extract articles and news on unmanned aerial vehicles from online encyclopedias (including Baidu Baike (https://baike.baidu.com/) and Chinese Wikipedia (http://zh.wikipedia.org/)) and a news portal (i.e., Sina Military News (https://mil.news.sina.com.cn/)), respectively. The basic corpus and external extracted textual data compose our final corpus to information extraction.

The SpERT Model. SpERT is a joint instance and relation extraction model based on BERT [1]. This model adopts a span-based approach: any token subsequence (or span) constitutes a potential entity, and a relation can hold between any pair of spans [2]. The first reason why we choose this model is that it is a span-based model. Compared with the traditional models based on the BIO/BIOU labels, it can identify overlapping instances. For example, in the sentence "*Ford's Chicago plant employs 4,000 workers*", "*Chicago*" and "*Chicago plant*" are instances. However, the models using BIO/BIOU labels can only give each word one label, so in this situation, it will miss target instances. The second reason is that the core of this model is BERT, which has been proved powerful in many natural language processing tasks. The model mainly consists of three parts, i.e., span classification, span filtering and relation classification.

Span classification and span filtering are used to filter and identify instances. Relation classification is used for relation extraction. It has several advantages: 1) it is not influenced by the propagation errors of instance recognition, for it is a jointly extraction model; 2) SpERT only passes each input sentence forward once, and performs lightweight reasoning, which effectively reduces the computational load; 3) the downstream processing is simple for the use of instance classifiers and relation classifiers. These advantages make our information extraction more effective in extracting high-quality triples (Fig. 3).

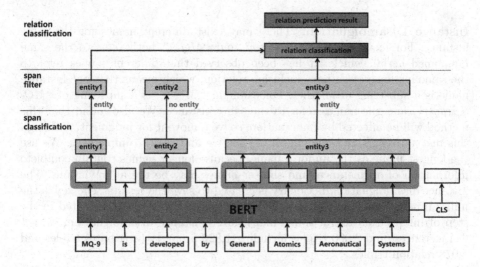

Fig. 3. The overall structure of our applied SpERT.

Instance and Relation Extraction. Instances and relations can be directly extracted with the SpERT model. In addition, we also regard instance property extraction as a task of instance relation extraction. For example, the property "wingspan" can be treated as a relation between an instance of unmanned aerial vehicle and a specific value of wingspan.

We utilize the SpERT model pretrained on our corpus. We label a small training corpus manually. Each training data is a single sentence after tokenization, and target instances and their relations are labeled. Many kinds of word segmentation models are tried, such as HanLP (https://github.com/hankcs/HanLP), FoolNLTK (https://github.com/rockyzhengwu/FoolNLTK), and another tool pkuseg (https://github.com/lancopku/pkuseg-python). For HanLP, the result is influenced by the input content. The more you input, the better result you will get. The tokenization result of a paragraph is much better than a sentence, so it is not suitable for single sentence segmentation. The efficiency of FoolNLTK is low, so it is time-consuming to deal with the whole training corpus. Compared with FoolNLTK, the accuracy of pkuseg is almost the same but the efficiency is much better. Therefore, pkuseg is used as our word segmentation tool.

After tokenization of the training corpus, we train the SpERT model and adopt it to extract triples. In order to further fine-tune the model and extract more triples, we propose an iterative extraction strategy. There are three steps in each iteration for this proposed strategy. Firstly, we use the model to predict on the whole corpus. Then, we check the prediction results manually to prevent semantics shift. New extracted instances and relations are added. Finally, the correct prediction results are checked manually and used as the labeled training data for the next iteration. The same process is iterated until there is no new reasonable result after checking.

Instance Disambiguation. There may exist different names for the same instance. For example, "*MQ-9 reaper*" and "*MQ-9*" both refer to the same unmanned aerial vehicle. It has been observed that different names refer to the same instance often have inclusion relation, which means that one instance name is a substring of another. For example, "*MQ-9*" is a substring of "*MQ-9 reaper*", and the names refer to the same instance. We also found that this method will be affected by punctuation, so we remove it for judgment. Although this method seems quite simple, it is effective and easy to implement. We use the longest name as the uniform name, because longer names contain complete information of an instance, and shorter names may be the abbreviations. The instance disambiguation dictionary is created to save the results. The key is the uniform name, and the value is all the names of this instance extracted in the step of information extraction. Finally, after instance disambiguation, we get 644 instances, and 2,900 triples including 1,822 property (attribute) triples and 1,078 relation triples.

3.3   Knowledge Graph Visualization

In order to realize the visualization of the knowledge graph, we choose neo4j (https://neo4j.com/) as the platform. A part of our knowledge graph is shown in Fig. 4.

4   Evaluation of Knowledge Graph Construction

This evaluation task aims to find practical and effective techniques of domain-specific knowledge graph construction. There are two stages of this evaluation task including knowledge graph quality evaluation and knowledge graph usage evaluation.

4.1   Knowledge Graph Quality Evaluation

The stage of knowledge graph quality evaluation focuses on the quality of knowledge graph. In this stage, the built knowledge graph in the CSV format is submitted online and it will show you the score of the knowledge graph. The score is computed by a formula:

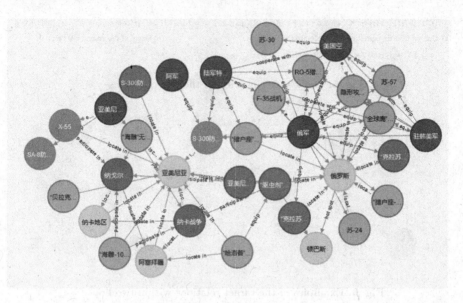

Fig. 4. A part of our knowledge graph.

$$ME = \frac{10\mu log_2^N}{\sigma} \tag{1}$$

where μ and σ are the average and variance of the number of relation triples that each instance exists in, respectively. N refers to instance number and ME is the evaluation score. According to the formula, if N and μ are bigger and σ is smaller, the score is higher. Thus, this metric expects that there are more instances in the knowledge graph and the instance relations are as average as possible for each instance. The score of our team is 274.74913, and we achieves the second place in this stage.

4.2 Knowledge Graph Usage Evaluation

The stage of knowledge graph usage evaluates the ability of solving practical problems by the built knowledge graph. There are two questions given by the evaluation task. We solve both questions by writing Cypher queries on the knowledge graph.

The first question is finding all the relations of power system instances and radar instances within two hops. We first find these two kinds of instances in classes "*equipment*" and "*facility*". We then search all the relations within two hops by a simple query given in Fig. 5 (a). Figure 6 shows the examples of the query results, i.e., the target relations within two hops.

The second question is to describe the situation of cooperation through knowledge graph. Every team have to submit a document describing how to solve the problem in detail. We first query all the "*cooperate with*" relations in the knowledge graph, using the query given in Fig. 5 (b). Besides, we also

MATCH (a)-[r1]-(n)-[r]-(p:'XX'{'name':'YY'})   RETURN n,r,p,a,r1   MATCH p=()-[r:'cooperate with'] →() RETURN p

(a) Query of the first question. 'XX' refers to the class name   (b) Query of the second question.

and 'YY' represents the instance name.

Fig. 5. Our Cypher queries on the two questions.

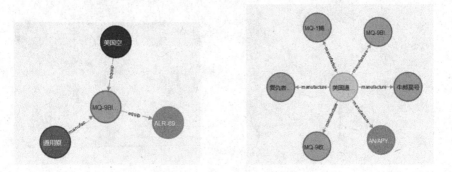

Fig. 6. Examples of the target relations within two hops.

analyze different kinds of unmanned aerial vehicles and equipments which took part in the same war. For example, in 2020 Nagorno-Karabakh War, Azerbaijan exploited several kinds of unmanned aerial vehicles, including *"Berakta TB2"*, *"Halop"* and *"Orbit-1K"*. These unmanned aerial vehicles have the experience of cooperating with each other, and we describe this situation in the document. Finally, our team achieves the third place in this stage.

4.3 Our Strengths

Our team achieves good performance in this evaluation task, which proves our framework is effective. We summarize three reasons for such a good performance. Firstly, the SpERT model we applied is a joint extraction model to avoid the propagation errors of instance recognition, and a span-based model to overcome instance overlapping problem. Secondly, we propose an iterative extraction strategy to obtain as many triples as possible. Although there exists a semantics shift problem, we manually check the prediction results to avoid negative effects. This strategy greatly increases the number of triples we extract. Thirdly, the schema is reasonably designed and comprehensive which helps us solve practical problems.

5 Conclusion

In this paper, we propose a framework to construct a domain-specific knowledge graph from textual data. We construct an unmanned aerial vehicle knowledge graph using SpERT and we achieve the second and the third place in the two stages of the evaluation task (i.e., military domain-specific knowledge graph construction for military unmanned aerial vehicles) in CCKS 2021, respectively.

In the future, we plan to design a question answering system based on the built knowledge graph, in order to promote the practicality of our unmanned aerial vehicle knowledge graph.

Acknowledgement. This work is supported by the National Natural Science Foundation of China (Grant No. 62006040), and the Project for the Doctor of Entrepreneurship and Innovation in Jiangsu Province (Grant No. JSSCBS20210126).

References

1. Devlin, J., Chang, M.W., Lee, K., Toutanova, K.: BERT: pre-training of deep bidirectional transformers for language understanding. arXiv preprint arXiv:1810.04805 (2018)
2. Eberts, M., Ulges, A.: Span-based joint entity and relation extraction with transformer pre-training. arXiv preprint arXiv:1909.07755 (2019)
3. LiuQiao, L., DuanHong, L., et al.: Knowledge graph construction techniques. J. Comput. Res. Dev. **53**(3), 582 (2016)
4. Miwa, M., Bansal, M.: End-to-end relation extraction using LSTMs on sequences and tree structures. arXiv preprint arXiv:1601.00770 (2016)
5. Miwa, M., Sasaki, Y.: Modeling joint entity and relation extraction with table representation. In: Proceedings of the 2014 Conference on Empirical Methods in Natural Language Processing (EMNLP), pp. 1858–1869 (2014)
6. Pawar, S., Palshikar, G.K., Bhattacharyya, P.: Relation extraction: a survey. arXiv preprint arXiv:1712.05191 (2017)

Author Index

Printed in the United States
by Baker & Taylor Publisher Services